REFLECTIONS

A GLIMPSE OF
BRITAIN
1930s - 2020s

Memoirs of
Ivor Hodgson

Grosvenor House
Publishing Limited

This book is published by
Grosvenor House Publishing Ltd
Link House
140 The Broadway, Tolworth, Surrey, KT6 7HT.
www.grosvenorhousepublishing.co.uk

A CIP record for this book
is available from the British Library

ISBN 978-1-80381-163-5

Foreword

Our dad, Ivor, has a wonderful gift for recalling events through history and telling the tales as if you were reliving them. His words describe the nation's feelings, as well as his own vivid memories, and put you back in the period. You sense the spirit of the times and all its emotions, good and bad. He notices so much, from the madness of some human decisions made in the last 90 years, to the sheer beauty and wonderment of others. It's a nostalgic, entertaining, and informative reflection.

Chris & Martin Hodgson

Acknowledgements

I'd like to give credit to the following people for their help with the production of my book.

Firstly, my two sons, Chris and Martin, who encouraged me to write and supported me from the start in writing my articles for *The British Touch* newsletter.

My three grandchildren, Nicole, Laura and Michael, who have helped in no small way in providing ideas for my book, with Nicole and Michael designing and creating the cover, and Laura who helped to edit my words.

I have spent many hours, days, weeks and months writing my story and providing the photographs, so I finish by adding my thanks to my wife for her forbearance and, sometimes stretched, patience.

Introduction

It's only natural for parents to relay events of their own lives to their children and I had been writing my recollections and insights into my past for a while as a personal blog. My eldest son, Chris, is the owner of a shop called *The British Touch* in Ontario, Canada. He sells all things British and has built the shop into a very successful business, providing the many expats in the area and Canadian locals with British sweets, treats, memorabilia and a good dose of nostalgia, too. He advertises his business by sending out a regular newsletter via email to inform his many customers of his stock, plus any upcoming sales and new items arriving at the shop. To help him in this venture, he asked me if I would contribute a regular article. Naturally, I was glad to help. I decided to call these articles *Ivor's Insights*. My articles were not only stories of my life, past and present, but also provided my thoughts and reflected upon past and current affairs in Britain. With all due modesty, I'm pleased to say that my words were well-received, bringing very favourable feedback. The interest in my articles eventually led to some readers asking if I had considered writing a book of my life story. This was very flattering and, after careful consideration, I decided to give it a try. I collated all those glimpses I'd written about and added a few more, which collectively provided the inspiration for this book.

My story provides my insights on a life of love, laughter, tolerance, and wise direction from my parents and siblings. My reflections are often happy, with some challenging and sad times, too. I reflect on how, significantly, as a small boy, I survived the Second World War, including my evacuation from London to avoid the bombing. I also reflect upon my diverse interests in music, sport, the Boys' Brigade, my National Service in the RAF, theatre, travelling (particularly caravanning and cruising) and photography.

Firstly, let me assure you this will be no masterpiece of prose, or a bestseller. Please bear with me as I attempt to relay some of the events – good, bad, big, small, interesting, boring and downright unbelievable – I've lived through, plus mistakes I have made, which I've tried not to repeat in my 90 (so far!) years. The world is mad, violent, intolerant, prejudiced, materialistic and ever-changing but, at the same time, it's also wonderful and beautiful.

Part 1
1930s

Chapter 1

In the Beginning

My parents, Herbert and Rebecca Hodgson, were born in London during the 1890s, both coming from ordinary working-class backgrounds. However, my father became regarded as one of the great printers of the 20th century. In 1926, he worked alongside T.E. Lawrence, better known as Lawrence of Arabia, in printing Lawrence's memoirs, *Seven Pillars of Wisdom*. This inspired my father to write his own memoirs, *Impressions of War*, published in 2010. Such inspiration, as well as the response to my newsletter articles, led me to writing my own memoirs.

Because of my somewhat hazy and limited knowledge of my early days, it is very fortuitous for me that I could draw on my father's memoirs as well as the help of my siblings (as I began writing my story some years ago) for any points of uncertainty I encountered.

Although my parents were Londoners, my story begins with my arrival into this world in Bettws Cedewen, Mid Wales, on 17th December 1931. I was the youngest of five children – four boys and one girl.

The blinding snowstorm on the night of 17th December 1931 had no mercy on the lone cyclist battling his way through the dark, on leafy, deserted lanes from the small village of Bettws Cedewain in Montgomeryshire (now Powys). The snow-covered figure, who was probably thinking, "What a night to have a blizzard," was my father, Herbert Hodgson. Frantically striving to keep his bike wheels upright and in a straight line, he desperately battled against the elements to make the two-mile journey to inform the local midwife that his pregnant wife had gone into labour earlier than expected, and therefore her services were urgently required. Within minutes there were two determined cyclists battling through the snowstorm on this labour of love back to Bettws and, thankfully, they made it just in time for my arrival. Thus, I became the fifth and last child born to Herbert and Rebecca Hodgson.

The first child born was my eldest brother who was christened Herbert (Bert) after Dad, followed by my sister Lillian (Lily) and she was followed by Bernard. As the fourth and fifth members of the family were born in Bettws, it was decided that they should have Welsh names so, in 1930, David (Daffyd) arrived followed by me, Ivor (Ifor), 18 months later.

My parents were both Londoners, Dad from Camberwell and Mum from Peckham. My father served his apprenticeship as a machine minder in the printing trade and worked as such up until the outbreak of the First World War. Like thousands of others, he immediately joined up and became a soldier in the $1/24^{th}$ (County of London) Battalion of the Queens's Royal Regiment

(West Surrey). After initial training he was sent to France and, despite serving on the Western Front, he somehow survived the war and returned to London and his printing work in 1918. He always considered himself just an ordinary bloke and one of the lucky ones to have survived the war but, unfortunately, he, like thousands of others, had horrific memories of trench warfare lying dormant in his subconscious mind, only for them to occasionally resurface and disturb his sleep with the terrifying sounds and vivid images of the death and destruction he witnessed. These nightmares haunted him for the rest of his life.

The Way to Wales

My father, who was a staunch believer in social and work justice, joined the Labour Party and was a member of the Printing Union for many years. It was the Printing Union who he turned to for help when he resumed his printing career after the First World War and work was hard to find. As the country was still recovering from the war, Dad would cycle each day to the Union headquarters in Blackfriars, London, seeking any available work. Sometimes he got a few days of work and other times he could be very lucky and get a week's employment.

This financial uncertainty continued until one day in 1923, when the Union sent him to an address in Westbourne Terrace in the Paddington area of London. This event would turn out to be (after the war) his next life-changing event, which subsequently changed the lives of his family, too. The work he was offered was to print the first (subscribers only) copy of T.E. Lawrence's book *Seven Pillars of Wisdom*.

No more would he be grateful for just a few days' work, this mammoth task would not only enable him to meet and work alongside Lawrence, it also kept him employed for the next three years. When the book was finished in 1926, Dad was temporarily out of work until, once again through the Union, he was introduced to another man who also had a big influence on his life. This man was Robert Maynard, one of the best artists of the day and the controller of the Gregynog (pronounced Gree-gun-ogg) Press in Mid Wales.

Maynard offered Dad the post of pressman. This invitation came out of the blue and demanded very careful thought by both Dad and Mum. After all, they were true cockneys through and through and the thought of moving the whole family (three children at that time) from their home in London to Wales, a country with a completely different environment and culture, was a decision not to be taken lightly.

After deep discussions between Dad and Mum, plus Robert Maynard, it was agreed that Dad would accept the post for a one-month trial period. So, with some trepidation of leaving Mum and his family in London, Dad took the train from Paddington to Aberystwyth and onto Newtown, where he was met by a chauffeur-driven Rolls-Royce which took him to Gregynog Hall where the Press was housed.

The one-month trial period was very successful, and Dad signed a three-year contract for a 48-hour working week at £4 and 10 shillings weekly wage. This exceeded the average £3 a week he had been receiving in London.

Making the Move

After suitable accommodation in nearby Bettws Cedewain was found, Dad returned to London to make the necessary arrangements for the whole family to leave the big smoke and move to this completely new world – one of clean air amid the green hills of the Welsh countryside. This was the world into which my brother David and I were born in 1930 and 1931 respectively.

The village of Bettws Cedewain (pronounced Bet-us-cur-dow-n) is set in idyllic surroundings amidst the welcoming singing hills of Mid Wales. At the time of my birth, the village consisted of about a dozen houses, two inns, two shops (one a Post Office), a working mill, a blacksmith, a tailor's workshop, a cobbler's shop, a wheelwright's shop, a stone church dominating the village, a school, a village hall, a small workshop-garage with one petrol pump and a stone bridge over a river. The two inns, the New Inn and The Talbot, were run by two villagers, one of whom was the wheelwright and the other worked in the mill.

In later life, my four older siblings would often recount their memories of Bettws and then register their surprise, amazement and even mock indignation because I couldn't remember or share their memories. I would be dismissed for being 'too young' to remember. It's quite true because I must admit that my only memory of living in Bettws is of the small stream at the back of our house. In my defence, I was only four and half years old when we left Bettws. I suppose that's what becomes of being the youngest of five.

The Gregynog Press was world-famous for its fine art printing and it employed only the very best artists, engravers and bookbinders of the day. Dad's printing expertise found its zenith whilst enhancing this amalgamation of such talented and creative people from 1927-1936, so much so that he was regarded as one of the finest printers of the 20th century.

In addition to his magnificent printing skills, Dad was also a musician, playing the piano and mandolin banjo (not at the same time of course). This talent led him to form a dance band which he called *The Venetian Dance Band*. They were very successful and in great demand playing at dances, weddings and parties in Bettws and the surrounding villages.

I think it's no exaggeration to say that Dad and Mum's decision to move to Wales turned out to be, after the First World War and the Lawrence of Arabia experience, the third pivotal period of their lives. The saying 'all good things must end' came true for us all in 1936, when Dad and Mum realised that with a growing family and the lack of suitable work opportunities around the Bettws area, apart from agricultural employment, it was time to leave this idyllic setting and move back to the London area.

Chapter 2

London Calling

The Big Smoke Awaits

In 1930, Robert Maynard, the controller of the Gregynog Press and the man who had employed Dad in printing in the first place, announced that he was resigning his post and leaving the Press to set up his own business, The Raven Press in Harrow Weald, Middlesex. During my father's time at the Gregynog Press he had built up such a happy working relationship with Maynard, that he told Dad to contact him if ever he decided to leave the Press and move back to London. Dad remembered Maynard's words so, when in 1936 he and Mum also left Bettws, he moved the family to Pinner near Harrow, and went to work for Robert Maynard.

As is the case with my cloudy memories of Bettws, it is the same regarding Pinner. What little I know about it has been gained from family conversations and my dad's memoirs. Suffice to say that we moved to 65 Pinner Hill Road, a modern semi-detached council house which had a lounge, dining room, a kitchen and cloakroom downstairs, and three bedrooms and bathroom upstairs.

For the first time we had a bathroom – instead of bathing in a tin bath filled with kettles of hot water – and electric lighting and power. Naturally, my brothers and I felt it necessary to check out this novel device by frequently switching the lights on and off, much to the annoyance of our parents. We also had one of the new (at the time) electric-powered radiograms which was housed within a beautifully finished wooden console that was such a piece of furniture in itself, it was afforded pride of place in the room.

The Joy of Cinema

Our move to Pinner was also the period when cinemas were spreading like mushrooms throughout the country. Pinner had the Langham and in nearby Northwood Hills there was an Odeon, as well as the Essoldo in Northwood. A weekly visit to the pictures was a way of life for millions throughout Britain around that time. The children were well catered for with suitable films shown every Saturday morning. There would be cartoons such as crime-busting heroes Flash Gordon and Superman. However, the most popular films were probably Westerns. Sometimes, cowboys such as Buck Rogers, Tom Mix and Hopalong Cassidy would be chasing bank robbers and prairies would echo with the sound of thundering hooves, which was watched with animated excitement. Another familiar scene was a wagon train being surrounded by marauding Indians and, when all seemed lost, the US cavalry would come galloping to the rescue. This would bring cheers and screams from the children in the audience.

One scenario which annoyed me was when the Sheriff and his posse would arrive at the bandit's hideout and the Sherrif would say to one member of his posse, "You stay here and the rest of you come with me." Now, I always felt that this was a little unfair. I can imagine the man told to stay behind thinking to himself, Why is it always me who has to stay behind and miss all the fun?

The Saturday morning films were so vivid and realistic that it was usual for us to exit the cinemas not as young boys, but as cowboys or soldiers chasing Indians. We fired imaginary guns at each other as we tore up the aisles and returned to the reality of our life in Middlesex. It's amazing when one looks back to that period and realises how wrong and misguided it was that children – as well as adults – were brainwashed into thinking that Native Americans were blood thirsty savages, riding the Great Plains attacking wagon trains and scalping any white people they captured.

Of course, we mustn't forget the last film shown each week, the serial film, which always ended with the hero facing certain death, hanging from a cliff top for instance, which meant we had to return next week to find out what happens next. Naturally, being the hero, he always found a way out of the predicament and survived, only to face another cliffhanger ending which forced you to return again the following week and so on, until, finally, the conclusive ending was shown to make way for the next serial and the whole rigmarole started again.

London Life

Meanwhile, from my parent's point of view, the new house at Pinner was Xanadu compared with our small two-bedroom cottage in Bettws. The move from Wales back to the London area was not only to benefit us children's education and my parent's work prospects, but it also had the added bonus of it being viable for my mother to visit her own mother and sister in London. She did this by catching a tube train at nearby Hatch End station straight through to Elephant and Castle. From there, it was a penny tram ride down the Old Kent Road to her mother and sister's house in Marcia Road, Peckham, just around the corner from the Dun Cow pub.

Life was good, but another change was necessary in 1938, when Robert Maynard announced that due to his business expanding, he needed bigger premises. He found this in Alperton near Wembley. Although Dad had been a keen cyclist all his life, he decided that the distance from Pinner to Alperton was a road (or two) too far for him to cycle daily, so we upped sticks once again and moved to 102 Rydal Crescent, Perivale. This time, the house was a modern three-bedroom terrace with bow windows and was privately owned. Something that surprised and, as a lifelong cyclist, pleased Dad was that the house was near one of London's new roads, Western Avenue, which had cycle tracks on each side of the road!

Anyone who knew Perivale at this time will no doubt remember the large Hoover factory (long gone) on the Western Avenue to the left of Rydal Crescent, and another factory named Peerless Factory at the opposite end. I have fond memories of the Hoover factory because, one year, as a six-year-old, I was invited to the traditional Christmas party they put on for the local children. Jellies, trifles, ice cream and all the cakes you could stuff in – plus a few more you shouldn't have. There were games, crackers, prizes, balloons; you name it, they provided it. When Hoover eventually stopped this annual treat, it left a big 'vacuum' in the children's lives, I can tell you.

I remember the 'Stop Me and Buy One' ice cream man who rode his three-wheeler bicycle around our streets. His bicycle had a wooden cabinet attached to the front which contained a variety of ice creams and ice lollies. Everyone, especially the children, would rush out, a penny in their hand, and accept his invitation with relish. Another welcome street visitor usually arrived on Sunday afternoon. This was the muffin man, who sold his wares from a tray carried on his head. As electric toasters weren't so readily available in those days, we would stick our toasting fork into each muffin and toast them one at a time over an open coal fire. The memory, and taste, of those muffins, especially when they were consumed around the fire on a cold winter's afternoon, is recalled with great fondness. Other street vendors in those days included a man we called a rag and bone man, who called out, "Any old iron?" as he drove his horse and cart down each road. If you had any old bits of iron, old clothes or other paraphernalia you wanted to dispose of, he was your man and, if you were lucky, he would give you a few pennies for them. Another long-gone caller I remember is the knife-sharpening man. He would have a knife grinding stone with him and for a small payment would sharpen any kitchen knives in need of it.

By this time, my eldest brother, Bert, had followed Dad into the printing trade, joining him at the Raven Press in Alperton. My sister, Lily, went to work in Perivale at Sanderson, the well-known wallpaper manufacturers. It was there that she was destined to meet a man who would eventually change both their lives for ever.

When I was six years old, I contracted scarlet fever and was taken into Clayponds Isolation Hospital in South Ealing. Due to the high risk of contagion of my condition, no visitors were allowed any direct contact with me, all they could do was to peer at me through a window. My only recollection of this illness is the fuss bestowed upon me by the rest of my family when I eventually recovered, and was discharged and taken home.

In 1938, there were ominous signs emerging from Europe that Adolf Hitler was causing much unrest by spreading his Nazi doctrine throughout the continent. The threat of another war so soon after the horrors of the First World War (the war to end all wars) was worrying to say the least. But, as always, life must go on and our family continued living in the relative suburban peace of Perivale. We even had a holiday that summer when Mum and Dad took us to sample the seaside delights of Margate.

Around this time, J. Lyons Corner House tea shops were familiar sights throughout the country. The company had a sports sheet which was printed on the back of the menus. This sports sheet changed every week and one of its features was to announce the name of the winner of a Dundee cake, which was awarded to someone who, in the opinion of the editor, had achieved an outstanding feat on the sports or athletic field. So, on our Margate holiday, Mum spotted a Lyons Corner House and as Mum and Dad studied the menu displayed on the window, they were amazed to read the name of the winner of the best sporting feat for that week. It was my brother Bernard, who, aged 11 years and 11 months at the time, had been chosen as a worthy winner for his outstanding cricket achievement whilst playing for Perivale School the previous season. The citation stated that he took 123 wickets in the season and recorded the highest one innings score of 52 runs. We were all 'over' the moon and Mum marched into the shop and explained about her son's sporting citation being printed on the back of the menu. She asked if she could keep the menu and, as her request was granted, the menu was taken, subsequently framed and spent many years proudly on display in the Hodgson family home.

Just after we returned from our adventure to Margate, the Dundee Cake was delivered to our house in a large round tin. Now there's no *point* in giving you a lot of *flannel* or trying to *cover* it up, so we have to *declare* that it tasted *out* of this world. We were all *bowled over*; *stumped* for words and our pleasure knew no *boundaries*. Howzat?

Dad's musical talent was passed down through his children, starting with my eldest brother, Bert, who received violin lessons in Wales, but by 1938, he decided to switch instruments and bought a trumpet. If anything,

Bert's musical ability surpassed Dad's and he quickly became very proficient in mastering the trumpet. Unfortunately, this venture didn't last. One day whilst out riding his motorcycle, he was involved in a road accident and suffered a cut to his upper lip which ended his trumpet playing days. But, undeterred by the incident, he went on to buy a saxophone and later, a clarinet. As with the trumpet, Bert's natural talent and dedication soon had the sound of the saxophone filling the house with many of the lovely melodies from the likes of Gershwin, Cole Porter, Irving Berlin and Jerome Kern.

1930s Events

Alas, those peaceful, innocent and melodic days were ended the next year when, on Sunday 3rd September 1939, Prime Minister Neville Chamberlain made his historic radio broadcast that ended with the words, "Consequently, this country is now at war with Germany."

Other events of interest in the 1930s include 1932 being notable for the first royal Christmas radio broadcast being made, when King George V addressed the nation. In November 1936, the BBC transmitted the world's first regular public television service from Alexandra Palace in London.

Sporting highlights included Britain's Fred Perry winning Wimbledon for the third consecutive year and Yorkshire cricketer Len Hutton making a world record innings score of 364 runs, which he achieved over 13 hours against Australia at the Oval.

Part 2
1940s

Chapter 3

The War Years

And So it Begins

I well remember that fateful September day in 1939. I was with my brother David and our gang playing near the railway lines, as one did in those days – we were probably trying to repel Sitting Bull and his Apaches at the Battle of the Little Big Horn. Suddenly, a woman appeared; she had an anxious look on her face and a sense of urgency in her voice as she instructed us to quickly get off home to our mothers. Wondering what on earth was more important than our historic battle, we mounted our trusty steeds (bikes) and high-tailed it back home.

The general opinion was that this war would be over in a matter of months. My eldest brother, Bert, was 19 and called up straight away. He went into the Royal Army Service Corps, taking his sax and clarinet with him. He thought it would break the monotony! Later he was shipped overseas and served with the Eighth Army under General, later Field Marshal, Montgomery in Egypt and Libya. Whenever it was safe to do so, Bert would take his clarinet and wander off to find a foxhole in the desert and practise. The odd squeak emanating from the clarinet would occasionally echo across the desert sand causing laughter from his comrades back in the camp. Talk about the Desert Song!

My father was appointed Air Raid Warden for our area which meant that every time the siren sounded, he would patrol the streets blowing a whistle and telling everyone to take cover. Not that there was anything to take cover from in those first few weeks, though. His work was slacking off at the Raven Press when, out of the blue, he was told by Robert Maynard that he had had a request from the Gregynog Press in Wales to loan him back to them to finish a couple of books. Maynard agreed to the request but said it was up to Dad. After much discussion with my mother and once all the safety precaution details were sorted out (such as should the air raids get worse then he would return home immediately), it was decided that Dad would go back to Wales for two to three months, returning every weekend.

During our time living in Perivale, it gradually became obvious that the lack of nearby shopping facilities was becoming too much of a burden on my mother. She would prepare breakfast and packed lunches for Dad, Bert and Lily, and then breakfast for Bernard, David and me. We three younger boys also came home for lunch and later for tea. After that, the three working members of the family came home to a cooked dinner. In those days we didn't have a fridge to keep food chilled, so Mum would have to walk to the local shop every day. As there was a bigger variety of shops in Greenford, it was decided to move there. So, in May 1940, we left Perivale and moved to 21 Wedmore

Road, Greenford, a three-bedroom semi-detached house with a bigger garden. This move made life a bit easier for Mum.

It should be said that during these days we had no television, computers, smart phones and the only tablets we had were the ones you swallowed for medical reasons. All the news came to us via the radio or wireless, or at the cinema with Pathé or Gaumont British newsreels. The BBC broadcasts were the lifeblood of communication to the country. Every news bulletin was eagerly awaited and listened to by all the family. In addition to providing this essential service, the BBC also raised the country's morale by broadcasting a variety of entertainment programmes. Millions gathered around their sets every Thursday evening at 8.30pm for their much-needed weekly ration of laughter.

The show that provided said comedy was called *ITMA* (*It's That Man Again*) and starred comedian Tommy Handley. To hear a recording of that show today sounds very old-fashioned and to be truthful a bit corny but, believe me, it was a life saver in those dark and frightening days. There were plenty of programmes dedicated to popular and classical music, too. One programme which was broadcast twice daily was called *Music While You Work*. This was a happy-go-lucky non-stop medley of well-known popular tunes, which had the listeners singing along in their homes, offices or in the factories. One hit song of the time was *Deep in the Heart of Texas*. After the first eight words – the stars at night are big and bright – were sung, you clapped your hands four times and sung the next line, deep in the heart of Texas. This clapping of the hands was a recurring feature of the song which was fine until, in some factories, instead of clapping, the workers would pick up their hammers and bang out the four beats on their benches or machines and cause damage, which didn't amuse the management. Another popular show was *Workers' Playtime*. This was broadcast at lunchtime from a factory 'somewhere in England' (this was a phrase deliberately used to avoid the enemy knowing exactly where it was coming from). The show was sent out live and the comedian would always find out in advance the name of the manager or foreman of the factory and use it in some comical way, bringing forth laughter and good-natured jeers from the workers.

The other star who must always be remembered was singer Vera Lynn. Many people thought her voice to be a bit 'slushy', but personal taste should not be allowed to detract from the wonderful work she did. As the 'forces sweetheart' she regularly broadcast on the BBC with her programme *Sincerely Yours*, and travelled overseas to entertain the troops, particularly into Burma, to sing for what was called 'The Forgotten Army'. She was a vital link between the troops and their loved ones at home. I still enjoy listening to her singing those wartime recordings of *Yours*, *The White Cliffs of Dover* and *I'll be Seeing You* despite the fact that, like Churchill's stirring speeches, it takes me right back to those dark days.

In July 1941, the BBC introduced its new V for Victory sign. This brilliant idea took the form of the first four notes of Beethoven's Fifth Symphony, which was ironic to say the least, considering that Beethoven was German and now part of his music was being used against his own countrymen. The BBC broadcast these four notes to occupied Europe and it proved to be a great morale booster, particularly to the resistance workers, giving them encouragement and also engendering a spirit of defiance to the enemy. This resulted in the workers chalking up V signs on doors and walls.

After the tragedy of the Dunkirk evacuation in 1940, air raids became a nightly occurrence. Due to my father's three-month period away working in Wales, he found on his return that he had lost his warden's post, but he quickly stepped in and became a fire watcher both at work and in our street. This involved watching out for incendiary bombs which resulted in fires.

Air Raids and Rationing

We were allocated a corrugated iron Anderson air raid shelter which was installed in our back garden. A hole approximately two and a half metres by two metres wide and one and a half metres deep was dug out, a concrete floor laid in the bottom and 100mm thick concrete walls lined the sides. The superstructure of the two longitudinal sides of the shelter consisted of two-metre-long sheets of corrugated iron with curved ends which were bolted together to an arch. The ends of the shelter were plain sheets of corrugated iron with an opening at the front for access. The earth from the hole was then backfilled up and around the superstructure. Bunk beds that would sleep four children were supplied. Any other furniture had to be found by the householder. This was all fine except for the fact that we had to share this shelter with our neighbours, Lou Cordon, his wife, May, daughter and son. This meant that the five children had to cram themselves into the two bunk beds whilst the four adults made do with any chairs small enough to fit into the space. I remember the air raid siren wailing out its mournful sound every evening at around 6.45pm. My father would just have time to get home from work and have something to eat, and then we'd all descend to our hole in the ground until morning. We had to find something to act as a door to cover the access opening at the front of the shelter. This was solved by sacrificing our slate bedded billiard table which did the job well. It thankfully received no bombs throughout those raids.

Every morning we kids would look for shrapnel which may have fallen in the street from the overnight raid. We collected it as souvenirs, the bigger the better, some pieces were so jagged the thought of the damage they could, and did, do was frightening. My mother used to warn us of these dangers and told us to stop collecting it. The ironic thing about all of these nightly raids was that our neighbours had an old lady lodger who refused to take any shelter. In true Churchillian spirit she declared that Hitler wasn't going to make her leave her bed at night. She survived the war in her nice warm bed!

On this nightly shelter ritual there were occasions when things quietened sufficiently during the night for the two men, my father and our neighbour, Lou, to venture outside the shelter into the garden on the pretence that it was just for a 'look around to see everything was in order.' Just what they would do if things weren't in order we never, thankfully, found out. Suffice to say that on these occasions, after a couple of minutes, the sound of a bottle opening and liquid being carefully decanted into a glass was heard. This delicate operation was followed by our neighbour saying in hushed tones, "Cheers Bert, all the best," a toast reciprocated by my father with, "Cheers Lou, same to you." You certainly couldn't blame them for having a few beers and a smoke (usually Woodbines, Players Weights or Park Drive) not knowing if each drink or smoke would be their last.

These day and night bombing raids were so common that it set a pattern which became a normal way of life for many people throughout the country. Life and work had to go on. The men would go off to work every day and hope that their loved ones, to say nothing of their houses, would still be there upon their return. Everyone was issued with a gas mask. This was stored in a cardboard box or a round tin which had to carried with you at all times. Windows in all buildings had to be completely blacked out at night so as not to emit any chink of light which could help guide an enemy aircraft. Air Raid Precaution Wardens (ARP) would patrol the streets and if they spotted a light anywhere, they would shout out in a loud voice, "Put that light out!"

We were lucky that, as Greenford is about 10 miles west of London, we were spared the terrible bombing raids they and other big cities of Britain experienced. We had a shock one day when one of our own anti-aircraft shells fell on Wedmore Road, but no one was hurt. The worst we had was when a land mine – a large bomb dropped by parachute from German planes – destroyed a local pub called The Load of Hay and killed the family owners. My father remembered seeing the remains of the parachute hanging from the trees surrounding the piles of rubble.

I remember sometimes on my way to school the air raid siren would sound just as I was approaching the entrance. I would quickly turn round and, being young and quite fleet of foot, would tear back home hoping for a day off school. This ploy was sometimes viewed with suspicion by my mother, who would doubt my protestations that I was only just around the corner when the siren sounded. Sometimes it worked, but on other occasions just as I arrived home, panting and puffing a bit, the All-Clear siren would sound and all my efforts came to nothing as I was packed off back to school. Rotten old Hitler, or words to that effect, come to mind. Of course, if we were already in school and the siren sounded, we were marched to the underground air raid shelters in the school grounds and continued our lessons there until the All-Clear siren sounded.

Another hardship we all endured was rationing. In January 1940, due to the German submarines attacking many British ships bringing food and other supplies to Britain, the government were forced to introduce some sort of rationing. This entailed each adult being issued with a ration book which you presented to each shopkeeper when purchasing any product (there were no supermarkets in those days). The shopkeeper would cross off the appropriate coupon in the book accordingly.

Here is a short list of some of the food stocks which were rationed: Bacon, sugar, butter, meat, tea, cheese, tinned tomatoes, rice, eggs, peas, canned fruit, biscuits, breakfast cereals, milk, dried fruit, cooking fat, jam. A typical ration per person per week was: Butter 2oz, margarine 4oz, bacon 4oz, sugar 8oz, milk 3 pints (sometimes only 2 pints), meat – to the value of one shilling (approximately equates to 5p today), cheese 2oz, one fresh egg, dried egg – one packet every four weeks, tea 2oz, jam one pound every two months, sweets 12oz, also every four weeks. I remember visiting our local sweet (candy) shop with our ration coupons and trying to make up our minds as to what to buy and working out if it would last until we were able to get any more. One of my favourite chocolate bars was Fry's Chocolate Sandwich. The name wasn't surprising because it was made up like a sandwich having a top and bottom layer of milk chocolate with a layer of dark chocolate in the middle. Unfortunately, this delicacy melted away many years ago.

In addition to the items on the above rationing list, everyone was allowed 16 points per month to use on whatever food items they chose. I remember the packets of dried egg powder which came from America. It was in a brownish coloured, waxy cardboard packet, bearing a picture of the stars and stripes on the front. One packet was equivalent to 12 eggs. The product was suitable for making omelettes or scrambled eggs and quite nice to eat as I remember. We also had Spam tinned meat from Argentina and whale meat called Snoek from South Africa. Of course, expectant mothers and all infants were entitled to more than the above rations.

The government encouraged everybody to grow their own food wherever possible. 'Dig for Victory' was the motto, which saw house lawns, flower borders and allotments turned into vegetable gardens. We benefited from all three, thanks to my father's efforts working in our garden, as well as tending to an allotment. I remember every house had 'pig' bin allocated which was for any scraps of food left over (which wasn't ever very much). This receptacle was collected weekly by the local council and its contents were fed to some hungry pigs somewhere. Our bin was often hauled into the middle of our road by us boys and served as a wicket in a game of cricket. Sometimes a figure of authority would appear and tell us off, forcing us to put the bin back in the garden.

Although rationing was sometimes difficult and stressful for the adults in particular, in later years when health experts looked back at the war time food rationing regime, they came to the conclusion that the general health of the public was far better in those days than subsequent years, when food stocks were plentiful with shops full of so many choices. Unfortunately, a lot of the choices contained excessive fat, sugar and salt, as well as chemicals and insecticides which subsequently led to a dramatic increase in cases of diabetes and obesity.

As well as food, other items such as clothes, paper, petrol, soap (one bar a month – "Hurrah!" said the kids) and washing powder were also rationed.

I remember in the kitchen, in an effort to eke out the meagre butter ration, mum would make her own substitute butter/margarine spread, don't ask me what the ingredients were, but it tasted fine and helped us through. Also, when making a beef stew with dumplings she would put in a couple of extra dumplings and when they were cooked, she would fish them out, drain off most of the gravy and then put some jam over them and feed them to we three, always hungry, boys, who devoured them with relish and gratitude. I carried the memory of this innovative and filling dessert into later years and when I was married, much to the surprise of my wife, I would occasionally ask her to put an extra dumping into the wonderful beef stews she makes so that I could cover it in jam and relive that wartime memory. I'm pleased to say it worked once or twice.

I can't say I will never know how on earth my mother coped with feeding and looking after all of us so well during those days of austerity, because I do know the answer. She was, like all mothers, always putting her family first. She may have been small in stature but what she lacked in height she more than made up for in stamina, dedication and love for her family. I should also add that, like many other women, she took a job working in a local factory, helping the war effort. We were so lucky to have such a strong lady as our rock and anchor.

As the youngest son, it was natural that some of my clothes were hand-me-downs from my brothers, but my mother would also visit jumble sales and find other suitable clothes for us all. I remember coming home from school at lunch time on Mondays and seeing the kitchen filled with steam with my mother up to her arms in soap suds, washing clothes in the boiler. As if that wasn't hard enough work, the clothes still had to be put through the hand operated mangle afterwards. But, being a Monday, Mum would usually have managed to keep some meat and vegetables left over from Sunday so I would have a slice of meat accompanied by lovely bubble and squeak for my lunch. Unfortunately, in time, this weekly hand-washing task affected Mum's hands so badly that she developed dermatitis. She was forced to apply the appropriate cream daily onto her hands and cover them with bandages to ease the suffering. This painful and debilitating condition couldn't go on, so my father bought Mum a washing machine which, if I recall correctly, was called a Swirl-lux. Thank goodness, as this innovation made her life a lot easier.

Evacuation to Devon

The air raids intensified, particularly during the Battle of Britain. It was thrilling for us boys to watch the Spitfires and Hurricanes engaged in a life-or-death dogfight with the German planes. The vapour trails left by the criss-crossing aircraft left beautiful patterns in the blue sky, quite the contrast to the deadly battle for survival above us.

My sister Lily decided that she wanted to 'do her bit' to help the war effort, so she joined the Auxiliary Territorial Service (ATS) and worked in London helping on what was called the Ack Ack guns. These weapons were deployed in an effort to shoot down the German planes attacking London. It was around this time that Ealing Borough Council sought to encourage the evacuation of children away from the London area to safer areas of the country. It was a voluntary scheme, but my parents thought it wise to send their three youngest; Bernard, David and me. Pupils at Greenford County School, which Bernard and David attended, were being evacuated, so my mother asked the headmaster if I could go along with them. He agreed, so, in October 1940, she took us all to the school and watched us board a coach (complete with our gas masks in their cardboard box over our shoulders) and leave Greenford for a secret destination. It was fortunate that Bert was home on leave at the time and was able to provide emotional support to Mum. Naturally, my parents found it very strange to return to a house now silent, devoid of the sound of family laughter and bustle. It was a couple of days later that an official letter arrived telling them that we were now being taken care of by a family in Torquay, Devon.

When our coach arrived at Torquay, all the children were offloaded and taken into a school. We were greeted by many local residents who were willing to take one or two evacuees into their homes. Of course, there were three of us, so we had wait until a family willing to take us was found. It was around 9pm when such a family arrived. We were then taken by car to the house of Mr and Mrs Hawkins, who had a young daughter and a grandmother already living in the house. Upon our arrival, Mrs Hawkins sat us down to have something to eat. All was fine until her daughter brought a cup of cocoa into the room and accidentally spilt some of it over Bernard's coat. Not a very auspicious start. We were very tired from our long journey and soon packed off to bed. David and I were not happy bunnies at all and, once in our room, we sat down and wrote a letter to Mum and Dad asking if we could come home! Needless to say, the letter wasn't sent. Bernard was fine and soon attended a local school, whilst David and I explored the local fields, enjoying a life of freedom for a few weeks. Anyway, our carefree life came crashing down when Bernard came home one day and told us that we were to report to school the following day.

In time, we settled into our new life in Torquay and enjoyed trips to the beach. David and I remember one particular day when I was standing on a rock in the sea, dangling a piece of string which had a small lead figurine of a farmer fixed to it (or so I thought), when tragedy struck. Why on earth I was doing such a strange thing I have no idea. It seemed a good idea at the time I suppose. Anyway, suddenly a big wave came crashing in and I was left with just a piece of string with Farmer Giles lost at sea! We often wondered where he ended up. (As I write this aged 90, I'm still wondering!)

Even though the many people who welcomed evacuees into their homes were recompensed by the government, it should be remembered that they deserve our thanks and recognition for the vital part they played in helping the war effort. Our landlady, Mrs Hawkins, had a strict method of food distribution at mealtimes. For instance, at teatime she would lay the table and point to the contents on each plate. It might be a plate with cakes on it and another plate with scones lying there invitingly, and a third plate containing slices of bread and butter. She would point to one of the cakes on the first plate and utter the firm instruction, "There's one of those each," and an instruction was issued on the next plate. When she reached the bread and butter plate she would show generosity and boldly declare, "There's two slices of bread each." Now, this was fine for Dave and me, but Bernard was a growing boy and needed much more sustenance. So, he resorted to creeping downstairs at night and raiding the kitchen for any tasty morsels he could find.

In 1941, my parents decided to visit us. They caught a night train that passed through Bristol. A German air raid on Bristol had just finished when they arrived. Several engines and carriages outside Bristol station were alight and there were palls of smoke around. This delayed them which resulted in them arriving in Torquay two hours late. It didn't matter, though, as we had a lovely day with them and, in an effort to take our minds off their necessary departure back home to London, they took us to the cinema where we saw *Gulliver's Travels*.

As time went on and the bombing raids eased, it was decided it was safe for us to return home. By this time, Bernard was 13 and wanted to stay. He wanted to change his billet and found one with a friend of his, but the lady couldn't take his two brothers. So, David and I left the green pastures and seascapes of glorious Devon – and a wet and never-to-be-seen again Farmer Giles – and returned to Greenford. I remember for our homecoming Mum had got a treat for our tea – a tin of pears, which were very rare. We were glad to be home again and soon adjusted to our old life with friends and familiar surroundings. I became interested in sport, particularly football, and saw my first professional football match when Brentford played Clapton (now Leyton) Orient at Griffin Park – Brentford won 4-2. I remember three of the Brentford players, goalkeeper Joe Crozier, and the two full backs; Bill Brown and George Poyser. Brentford and Queens Park Rangers (QPR) at Loftus Road were our local teams.

Chapter 4

The Peak of War

The Second World War was in full flight by the beginning of 1941. The absence of so many men into the forces caused the Minister of Labour, Ernest Bevin, to introduce plans to mobilise women to take on vital jobs in industry. There were already thousands of women in the armed forces, but now thousands more responded to the call to the home front. Whether single, married, widowed, young or old, the women of Britain proved that they were ready, willing and very able to more than do their bit for the war effort.

All American

In December 1941, Japan made their surprise attack on Pearl Harbour and America entered the war. The attack was a momentous occasion which President Roosevelt described as 'An act of infamy'. Winston Churchill, who had a close working relationship with Roosevelt (the President had sanctioned the supply of ships, guns and other weapons to aid Britain, but due to political pressures had held back from taking America into the war), immediately condemned this barbarous act and joined Roosevelt in declaring war on Japan. However, Churchill admitted that he was elated because, as we now had the colossal military strength of America behind us, the war was over!

After the Pearl Harbour attack, it wasn't long before Britain was 'invaded' by thousands of American troops. They were a welcome sight, particularly to the ladies and the children. Their smart uniforms and general easy-going nature made a refreshing change for the war-weary people of Britain. Some of the British servicemen were slightly wary and, to be honest, a little jealous due to the big difference between the wages of the American troops compared to the British. Their wages enabled the Americans to be generous, which they always were, giving nylon stockings, perfumes and lipsticks to the ladies, and dishing out chewing gum and sweets to the children, as well as putting on parties for them. It was fun for the children to ask the American soldiers, "Got any gum, chum?" The request was usually successful.

Another attraction the Americans brought was their accents. Whether from the Bronx area of New York City, the Southern States, or California, as far as we were concerned, they all sounded as though they were straight from Hollywood! People thought they lived either in big houses surrounded by white picket fences and drove big gleaming cars, or they lived on ranches with verandas where they'd sit in rocking chairs on the porch, sipping a mint julep.

American personnel were based all over Britain, but particularly in places such as Lancashire and East Anglia which, due to their flattish landscapes, provided ideal conditions for the Bomber bases used by the RAF and the United States Air Force (USAF). The RAF would carry out night bombing raids over Germany, whilst the USAF covered the daytime raids.

Before the arrival of the American forces, Britain had already called for help from its vast Commonwealth countries. Not that they needed much calling – Australia, Canada, New Zealand, South Africa, Rhodesia, India, Jamaica and many others had already rushed to our aid, as well as the already oppressed Poland, Czechoslovakia (now Czech Republic and Slovakia) and the Free French.

Living in Greenford, we saw and heard many American airmen from the base in nearby South Ruislip. We sometimes saw them travelling on underground tube trains, they were always smiling and friendly, particularly to the children, and we envied their demeanour.

It wasn't long before the attraction between the American troops and the British ladies grew, as the illusion of the American Dream strengthened. Many ladies were swept off their feet and this led to engagements and weddings between them and the General Issues (GIs), as they were called. Unfortunately, many of these GI brides were bitterly disappointed and disillusioned when they later left Britain to start a new life in America. They expected their new homes to be palatial, like the ones they'd seen in films, but many were run-down, small apartments or, even worse, a shack with terrible, if any, sanitary facilities. Sadly, this led to heartbreak and many subsequent divorces.

Dark Days

One of the biggest disasters of the war occurred on 19th August 1942. This was the ill-fated Allied raid on the French port of Dieppe. The raid was carried out in response to a request from Russia's leader, Josef Stalin, for the Allies to open a Second Front on the continent because his own troops were under extreme pressure fighting the Germans on the Eastern Front.

The Allied troops consisted of 5,000 Canadians, 1,000 British and 50 US Rangers. The Canadians had well over 3,000 casualties, of which there were over 900 dead with the rest wounded or taken prisoner. Whilst the British Commandos had the most military success of the raid, they still lost 275 men. In addition, there were many ships and planes lost in this disaster. It was total carnage, and if you've ever visited the port of Dieppe you will understand how easy it was for the German forces, high up in their vantage positions, to machine gun the troops as they landed on the beaches.

It was subsequently claimed by the military 'planners' that although the loss of life was regrettable, lessons were learnt regarding the best way for any troops to carry out future amphibious raids from England across the channel to France, which, of course, was what was done on D-Day in 1944.

By April 1943, massive preparations along Britain's south coast were underway with military vehicles, glider planes and thousands of British, Commonwealth and American troops assembling for the Allied invasion of Europe.

My wife, although only a schoolgirl at the time, was living between Southampton and Fareham in Hampshire and saw many of these troops, particularly Canadians, sleeping under their trucks and tanks ready for the big day. One night, during a severe air raid, some of these Canadian soldiers were commended for driving their burning armed vehicles away from their village base to minimise casualties.

On 17th May 1943, the daring Dam Busters raid by the RAF's 617 Squadron led by Wing Commander Guy Gibson took place. Their 'bouncing bombs', invented by Barnes Wallis, didn't inflict as much permanent damage to Germany's war production machine as had been hoped. Our casualties were high, but the sheer daring and inventiveness of the surprise raid certainly shook the enemy and did wonders for the Allies' morale. Sadly, 18 months later, Guy Gibson, who received the Victoria Cross for his part in the raid, was killed when his plane ran out of fuel and crashed near Steenbergen in the Netherlands.

D-Day finally arrived on 6th June 1944, when at long last the Allied invasion to free Europe from the tyranny of the Nazis began. A week later, on 13th June, the first V1 flying bomb landed on England. There are many claims as to exactly where it landed, from places such as Swanscombe in Kent, who claim one landed there at 3.41am, to London's Docklands area. I can still recall the chill that went through me when I heard the BBC news referring to these new 'pilotless' planes. As a 12-year-old I wondered how on earth a plane could travel without a pilot. I'll admit, it scared me a little. We eventually got used to the eerie sound of these 'buzz bombs' or 'doodlebugs' as they were named. They were capable of speeds up to 400mph and carried one tonne of high explosives. They were designed to run until they ran out of fuel, at which time they would stall and around 15 seconds later would crash down to earth, exploding on impact. At night, they emitted an orange flame as they went on their murderous missions. As long as you could hear the drone of the engine you were safe, but as soon as that drone stopped, you could only pray that the bomb wasn't heading your way. Because of this, they became known as 'Bob Hopes' – you bobbed down and hoped for the best. The sound of silence was deafening and frightening at the same time.

In July, the danger from these V1 attacks was so bad that parents in London once again decided to evacuate their children to the safety of the countryside. After having killed over 6,000 and severely injuring 18,000 people, the attacks stopped on 2nd September.

A short respite was followed by Hitler's final plan. This was the launching of his more deadly V2 rockets. These were capable of supersonic speed and flying at over 50 miles high. I believe Chiswick, in west London, received the first one on 8th September, killing three people and injuring 22. Unlike the V1, these machines had no engine droning to alert you of their presence. When they ran out of fuel, they just left the heavens and brought hell to earth without any warning. The heaviest casualties at one time was when 168 people died when a V2 landed on a Woolworths store in New Cross, London in 1944. But fortunately for us, these weapons were unreliable. Many either exploded on launching or they completely missed their target when they did come down. Nevertheless, of the 5,000 launched, about 1,000 reached Britain killing nearly 3,000 and badly injuring 6,000. The attacks finally ended on 27th March 1945, when the last one landed on a street in Orpington, Kent, killing 34-year-old Mrs Ivy Millichamp – the last British civilian to die from these silent killing machines.

Bittersweet Victory

On 8th May 1945, Germany surrendered and the war in Europe was over. This was followed by Japan's surrender on 15th August the same year, after America dropped two atomic bombs. These two historic days were named VE Day (Victory in Europe) and VJ Day (Victory over Japan). Although there was plenty of celebration all over the country, not everyone felt the euphoria. These were the people who had lost loved ones and still felt the loss too much. There were others who seemed to have forgotten how to have fun. There's one story of a lady who, in a fit of devil-may-care attitude, suddenly decided to put the kettle on and open a tin of pears she'd kept stored on a shelf!

Back in the dark days of 1940 when Britain was preparing for Hitler's army to invade, we wouldn't have dreamt this wondrous day of victory could be possible. Back then, the threat was so great that Anthony Eden, the Minister for War at the time, appealed for volunteers to join a new fighting force he planned for the home front. This force was to be called the Local Defence Volunteers (LDV). There was a huge response – many veterans from the First World War signed up. By the next day, a quarter of a million men had enlisted. The experience of these older men brought forth a little humour with them by suggesting some alternatives to the proposed name of this new force. For instance, they suggested that the letters LDV could mean 'Long-Dentured Veterans' or even 'Last Desperate Venture'. For me, the best (although maybe a little unpatriotic) suggestion was 'Look, Duck and Vanish!'. But none of these suggestions were implemented, as Winston Churchill decided this new fighting force was to be known as the Home Guard.

This name remained until actor and writer, Jimmy Perry (1923-2016), teamed up with BBC producer, director and writer, David Croft (1922-2011), in 1968 and brought one of the most successful television shows to our screens. Jimmy Perry had served in the Home Guard himself and decided to write a show based on his experiences. His original title was *The Fighting Tigers* but this was changed at the suggestion of the BBC Head of Comedy at the time, Michael Mills, to *Dad's Army* and the rest is history. The television series ran from 1968 to 1977 and is still showing repeat episodes today. There was also a full-length film version made in 1971. In my opinion, *Dad's Army* ranks alongside *The Good Life* and *Yes Minister/Yes Prime Minister* as the best television programmes ever made. They are beautifully written, superbly cast and acted, and they are still funny after all these years. As Captain Mainwaring might have said, "Well done, men. Britain is proud of you all. Wilson, tell the men to stand easy, that means you too Pike, stupid boy."

Other Poignant Moments

In March 1941, there was a shock announcement when it was disclosed that Germany's Luftwaffe planes had made an attack on Buckingham Palace. The planes dropped flares first to light up the Palace, before incendiary bombs were unleashed. Fortunately, they all missed the Palace. As Queen Victoria might have said, we were not amused.

On 9th May 1941, a gigantic breakthrough occurred when Royal Navy Destroyers – HMS Bulwark, Broadway and a Corvette, HMS Aubretia – attacked and captured the German submarine U-110. This in itself was a victory, but when the British Naval boarding party entered the submarine, they found something which was far more valuable. It was an Enigma Cipher machine, plus all the relevant codebooks relating to it. This was such a massive coup and one that Churchill and many historians estimated could have shortened the length of the war considerably, thereby saving thousands of lives. Later in my life story, when I was in the Royal Air Force (Signals), I was fortunate enough to see first-hand an Enigma coding machine which is on display to the general public at Bletchley Park in Buckinghamshire. If you ever get the chance to visit Bletchley Park – especially the ladies, of whom there were many working there, intercepting and decoding the hundreds of coded, top-secret messages being received daily – I urge you to do so. You won't be disappointed.

At about the same time as the above event, another shock arrived when Hitler's deputy, Rudolf Hess, surprised everyone by parachuting into Scotland. He broke his ankle upon landing in a field. He claimed he had a message for the Duke of Hamilton, whom he had met briefly at the 1936 Olympic Games in Berlin.

Although I heard about this on the BBC news, I had no idea that at the time of Hess's arrival there was a young lady living with her mother in a cottage on the Duke of Hamilton's Estate. The young lady was Ethel Stuart. She had gone out in the morning and upon her return, the place was swarming with police and troops. At first she was refused entry, but after she convinced them that she did live in the cottage she was allowed in. Ethel later decided to follow the example of many other like-minded women and joined the WAAF (Women's Auxiliary Air Force) where she worked alongside Wing Commander Kenneth Horne and Squadron Leader Richard Murdoch, two well-known popular radio artists. She also became a pen pal, writing to a soldier serving in the Middle East at the time. I know all of this about Ethel, for she eventually became my sister-in-law, through the fact that the soldier she wrote to was in fact my eldest brother, Bert!

As for Rudolf Hess, after his attempt at trying to make peace between Germany and Britain, he was judged to be mentally unstable and was jailed in the UK until

1945 when he was transferred to Germany and stood trial at the Nuremberg War Crimes Tribunal. He was found guilty of war crimes and imprisoned in Spandau jail until his death aged 93, on 17th August 1987. An interesting addition to the Hess story is that the father of the popular singer Olivia Newton-John was a code-breaker working at Bletchley Park during the Second World War and, according to Olivia, was responsible for the capture of Rudolph Hess!

Carrying On and Making Do

A fuel shortage hit Britain and the need to conserve water by using less when bathing was encouraged. Hotels were marking a 'Plimsoll' line on their baths, to mark the maximum depth the bath should be. People were asked to take fewer baths (which went down well with us kids!). The suggestion was that anyone taking a bath should not use more than five inches of water (that was about four inches more than we kids used anyway), and it was even suggested that shared baths were a good idea – a bit too far, in my opinion! It was reported that even the King followed these guidelines. Soap rationing meant that one tablet of soap per month was the normal ration, unless you were a coal miner, who got more. Shaving soap was not rationed but difficult to obtain, as were razor blades. The women had their own problems with shortages of cosmetics. This reduced them to using cooked beetroot juice for lipstick and soot for eye makeup.

The new utility cloth allied with a limit on the number of styles available, meant fashion was very plain and, due to the shortage of material, ladies' hemlines were always rising, which brought the colour back to the cheeks of many of the men. Ladies also suffered another blow when a ban was imposed on using any embroidery on nightclothes and underwear. The men had no double-breasted coats, no sleeve buttons and no turn-ups on trousers, all part of the rationing programme.

Anyone lucky or rich enough to own a car was only allowed petrol if their journey was essential. Driving for pleasure was banned. I remember the posters which clearly stated, Is your journey really necessary?

It was also around this time that a group of people met in Oxford. They were exploring ways of bringing supplies of food and clothing to war-torn Europe. This humanitarian idea blossomed and grew until eventually it became known worldwide as Oxfam (The Oxford Committee for Famine Relief).

At this stage of the war, the government released figures showing that the total cost of the war so far was over £9million. This was more than the entire cost of the First World War.

Some of the films I remember from this time are *Bambi*, *Mrs Miniver* (which won an Oscar) and *Holiday Inn*, in which Bing Crosby introduced Irving Berlin's song *White Christmas* to the world, which became the best-selling record of the time. Over the years it's proved impossible to keep old Bing down, as *White Christmas* is still a much-loved song played at Christmastime.

Bert's Return

When my brother Bert was with the Eighth Army in Egypt, he was chatting one day to another soldier, a Welshman from the Rhondda Valley, named Richard Price. Bert discovered that Richard also worked at Sanderson Wallpaper Manufacturers factory in Perivale and, furthermore, not only knew our sister Lily, but had taken her out a few times. Some time later, Richard was sent home on leave and called round to our house just to tell our parents of his chance encounter with Bert. As luck would have it, Lily opened the door to the surprise of her life. Well, all good stories should have a happy ending, and this one is no exception. Lily and Richard (known in the Hodgson family as Jack, although I don't know why!) later married and had two children.

Bert was demobbed in 1946 after six years of army life, four and half years of which were in the Middle East and North Africa. I remember the day he came home. After being in the Middle East for four and a half years he was obviously very brown, a fact Dave and I couldn't get used to, whereas Bert was totally surprised as to how much we, especially me, had grown taller. Dave was nearly 10 and I was under eight when Bert had last seen us. I remember he took us swimming the next day to the indoor public swimming baths at Ealing. Seeing him standing up on the top diving platform, all brown and a picture of health, made us feel very proud. Naturally, his safe homecoming was such a relief to my parents. I remember him and Mum hugging and crying and, later in the day, watching Dad cycling home from work and being greeted by Bert at the garden gate. It was a very happy and emotional time for all of us.

Because the war had interrupted Bert's working experience in the printing trade, he was very keen to get back and expand his knowledge, so eventually he got a job and settled back into civilian life. He also bought a motorcycle and I well remember one summer Sunday afternoon when he took me for a ride. As it was a warm sunny day, I left the house suitably dressed, only for Bert to order me back to the house to put on a sweater and a coat. All my protestations were in vain, so somewhat reluctantly I did what I was told and, suitably attired to pass inspection from Bert, I climbed onto the pillion seat and off we went from Greenford, past Uxbridge, heading out to Denham in Buckinghamshire. Later, we stopped for a rest and some light refreshments amid the peaceful and welcoming branches of Burnham Beeches, before heading back home. It was then that I, inexperienced in travelling on the pillion seat, had a rude awakening and realised why Bert had ordered me to don the appropriate warm clothing. The summer sun descended over the horizon, and my face was white with the bitter cold as I shrunk lower down the pillion seat and clung onto Bert for warmth and dear life.

Thank goodness that, in time, Bert decided to change to a car and bought a second-hand Austin 7. Being in the Royal Army Service Corp he gained a lot of mechanical experience working on lorry engines, so every evening after work he would use this knowledge to good effect by tinkering with his car, endeavouring to rectify any faults and ensure it was road worthy. For this nightly ritual he would often enlist my help to "Hold that" or "Hang on to this, Ive" (I was Ivor to my parents and my sister, but to my three brothers I was, and still am, Ive) whilst he grappled with some mysterious (to me) and obstinate engine component which refused to do what it was intended for.

Eventually, the big day dawned when Bert decided the car was ready for a trial run so, once again, I was detailed to help. This time there was no sitting on the back of a noisy motorbike and getting frozen in the process, instead I was promoted to chief pusher of this refurbished, gleaming Austin 7. With me at the back pushing like mad, Bert would wind down the window of the driver's door and put his hand through to steer the car as he also pushed whilst running alongside. When sufficient speed was gained, he would jump aboard and endeavour to jump start the engine. After quite a few fruitless attempts, Bert decided the car needed more speed before a jump start would succeed, so between us we pushed the car a couple of streets from ours and halfway up the next road which had quite a steep incline. The idea was that when we got to the halfway point up the incline, we would turn the car around and with Bert doing his running and steering act and me at the back pushing like mad, we would produce momentum of such velocity that the car engine would reluctantly leap into life when Bert applied the jump start action. Was it a success, I hear you ask. Well, up to a point, it was, but that point was reached when both head mechanic and chief pusher decided they were worn out and more tinkering was required to avert possible injury.

1940s Family Life

In 1943, my father had started working for the Hazel Press in Wembley. A year later, my brother David joined Dad at the same press where he became an apprentice compositor. I remember them telling the story of how, one evening when they were cycling home from work, they heard the dreaded drone of a doodlebug. When the noise suddenly stopped, they quickly abandoned their bikes and hit the ground. They were lucky because the rocket went on for another mile and hit the Glaxo factory in nearby Greenford. Another story I enjoyed hearing them recall related to concerns of where they used to have their daily lunch. During the war, the government had organised thousands of eating places which were named British Restaurant. For the princely sum of between nine pence and one shilling these emporiums provided, for your delectation, a very basic meal. The food was whatever was available during those hard times. Cold spam sitting sorrowfully amongst soggy and lumpy mashed potatoes floating in watery cabbage was often the only choice. This was usually followed by apple pie (which was mostly pastry – diners searched for some apple and found none or very little) covered with anaemic-looking custard made from powdered milk and water, which was an embarrassing excuse for custard. Those of a faint heart, or stomach, would reject the custard option whereby the server would call out, "Pie in the nude, is it?"

Bert joined Dad and Dave at the Hazel Press and, in a bid to further his career, started attending evening classes. My other brother, Bernard, not keen on entering the printing trade, was also attending night school three evenings a week following his chosen career to becoming a quantity surveyor. I was still only a mere lad of 12 whilst all this was going on, and would listen to all their stories at evening mealtimes.

Another emotional milestone came when Bert and his pen pal, Ethel, arranged to meet for the first time. Under the clock at King's Cross train station in London was the agreed rendezvous. It wasn't long before they, like millions before and after them, found out their answer to the question posed by Cole Porter in his song *What Is This Thing Called Love?* It's hard to define, it just happens, a feeling that this is the right person. They quickly knew that their letter-writing days to each other were over. They fell in love and were married in 1947 in the private chapel on the Duke of Hamilton's estate at Dungavel, near Hamilton, where Ethel had been brought up. My parents, plus Lilian, Bernard and of course, Bert, made the trip to bonnie Scotland. After their marriage, Bert and Ethel bought a house in Greenford and later had a daughter.

Meanwhile, Richard (Jack) Price was also now back in Civvy Street and returned to work at Sanderson in Perivale. He renewed his friendship with Lily and they too eventually married, also in 1947. They later had two children, plus grandchildren, and lived happily ever after, finishing their days together in Scone, Perthshire, Scotland, where their youngest son and his family still live.

Significant Stats

Referring back to Rudolf Hess for a moment, you might be interested to learn that on the same night (10th May) of Hess's arrival in Scotland, London suffered the worst air raid of the entire Blitz. The bombing carried on through the night. It is estimated that around 1,500 people were killed and 11,000 houses were destroyed. Bombs hit the Houses of Parliament; Big Ben was marked but continued to record the correct time. Both Westminster Abbey and Hall were hit, as was the British Museum and Waterloo Station. Even St Paul's Cathedral didn't escape – damage was done to the high altar, crypt and many of the stained-glass windows. But, as the saying goes, even in tragedy there's often humour, and that was vividly demonstrated on this night of horror with a typical example of British humour shining through. The well-known actor, Ballard Berkeley (the Major in Fawlty Towers), was a police special constable on this dreadful night of incendiary bombs raining down like fireworks. He recalled seeing a man put a steel helmet over one bomb and watched it become red hot, then white hot, before disintegrating. There was a newspaper seller standing stoically at his usual corner calling out the familiar cry of, "Star, News, Standard" but, as it was Cup Final day, he added the words, "Cup Final Result" to his call. Similarly, he witnessed a prostitute walking by, holding up an umbrella as she sang *Singin' in the Rain*. Thank goodness for such people in times of crisis.

Chapter 5

Leisure in My Youth

Pictures, Perfect

Around the time I returned from Devon, I rekindled my love of going to the cinema, or 'pictures' as they were generally known. I would pester my mum for the few pennies it cost. We had two cinemas in Greenford, one was the Granada – opened in 1938 by singer/comedian Gracie Fields – which cost the princely sum of sixpence to see two films, a 'B' film which was usually shorter in length, followed by the main feature film. Plus, there would be a cartoon and a newsreel, as well as a trailer advertising next week's films and, sometimes, arising from the depths at the front of the stage, a mighty organ would appear and the onboard organist would serenade the audience for about 15 minutes. The one I remember most was a very well-known organist called Robinson Cleaver. He was born in 1906 and at nine years of age played his local parish church organ. In the early 1930s, he was the solo organist at the Lonsdale cinema in Carlisle. He became the organist at the Regal cinema at Bexleyheath in 1934. He later played at other Granada cinemas in places such as Welling, Woolwich, Dartford and Tooting. His wife, Molly, was a pianist who would sometimes play duets with him. Robinson Cleaver died in 1987. I remember him for one simple fact, which is that as he ascended from the depths, he would be playing his signature tune – which I can still remember – and halfway through it he would insert a few bars of the sailor's hornpipe with one hand behind his back, just as sailors do when performing this traditional merry dance. Isn't memory a funny thing when one can remember such an inconsequential thing as that?

The Granada also had occasional talent shows which were presented by a chap called Bryan Michie. There was another man, named Carroll Levis, who presented a similar show called *Carroll Levis and his Discoveries*. When my brother Bert was home on embarkation leave, prior to being posted to the Middle East, he decided to enter the show. Naturally, Mum, Dad, Lily, Bernard, David and I, plus a few neighbours, all attended the show, and we were full of pride when Bert walked on in his army uniform with his saxophone and played three songs. I wonder if any readers remember these old numbers; *It's a hap-hap-Happy Day*, *It's a Lovely Day Tomorrow* and one of Bert's (and my) favourite songs of all time, Hoagy Carmichael's *Stardust*? You can imagine how we all felt when Bert won the contest. It really was a hap-hap-happy day for us all.

If the talent shows at the Granada were too much for you then you only had to walk around the corner and, lo and behold, there was another cinema – I use the term 'cinema' loosely, however, as this establishment was quite different in opulence to the Granada. The name on the front was The Playhouse, but it was better known locally as The Bughouse. Although the quality inside was not up-to-scratch (which meant we weren't itching to get in but itching to get out), it made up for it by only charging four pence to enter, and the films shown were of the same quality as the Granada.

Quite a few of the films we all saw during this time were war stories, and it's interesting to relive some of them nowadays as many crop up on television or can be purchased. Some I remember include; *Went the Day Well*, *Dangerous Moonlight*, *Millions like Us*, *Cottage to Let* (George Cole as a 10-year-old evacuee from London), *Hue and Cry*, *Next of Kin*, *One of Our Aircraft is Missing*, *In Which We Serve*, *The First of the Few* (Leslie Howard playing the part of the Spitfire's inventor, R.J.Mitchell), *Thunder Rock*, and to lighten the mood there was *Somewhere in Camp* (with the Northern comedian Frank Randle), *Abbot and Costello*, *The Three Stooges*, Disney cartoons like Donald Duck and Goofy, and the wonderful Will Hay with his side kicks, Graham Moffat and Moore Marriot.

If, when watching a film, an air raid suddenly occurred, a warning would appear on the screen informing the audience and anyone wishing to leave the cinema to do so whilst the film continued on the screen. At first, most people did leave and hurry home, but in time many became a little blasé and remained in their seats, often, quite ironically, watching war films!

In those days, films were checked by the British Board of Film Censors and given a rating according to their content. A rating of U (Universal) meant the film was suitable for all ages. A rating of A (Adult) signified a film was not suitable for children under the age of 12 unless accompanied by an adult. The last rating was H, which was used for horror films. Not my favourite. I think there was enough real-life horror going on all around us without paying money to see more.

When I used to pester my mother for the money to go to the pictures I was under 12 years of age, which meant if the particular film I wanted to see was rated an A film, the only way in was for me to hang around outside the cinema and ask any adult approaching the cinema entrance if they would take me in with them. This pleading question was delivered in my most polite voice accompanied by my dazzling smile as I offered my entrance fee up to them. How could it fail, I thought. After all, this approach was common practice amongst us boys and usually worked, but sometimes there would be too many of us hanging around outside the cinema with the same aim. In that case, it would be necessary to move further up the road from the cinema entrance and try to catch any person you thought might be heading for a night at the pictures, and approach them before your mates could. Many of these people were completely innocent, minding their own business and perhaps heading home or going shopping, and had quite a shock to be suddenly accosted by some boy asking to be taken into the cinema, when all they wanted to do was to get home and put their feet up!

Football Crazy

At this point, I think it's only fair to warn you that I shall divert to my ramblings on the football scene, so for anyone who wishes to skip these scintillating memories, I look forward to your return when the match is over, including extra time of course! After the war, my interest in football increased rapidly. I would spend hours in the street outside the front of our house, kicking a tennis ball against the wooden fence. The design of this fence was the angled, overlapping panel style, which meant the ball would come back at you from different angles. This necessitated learning to use either foot to return the ball back to the fence. My dedication to this practice bore fruit because throughout my subsequent football years – and I say this with all due modesty – I could use either foot with ease and not worry, or waste time, juggling it over to what is called 'my good foot'. I find it pathetic when some of the present-day so-called stars miss goal chances because they are fiddling about trying to get the ball onto their 'good foot'.

Another action I undertook after reading in a football manual that it was a good way to practise ball control, was to place a line of posts in the garden and dribble the ball around them without knocking any over. Now, as I didn't have any suitable posts, I improvised by using some of my dad's empty beer bottles. It was a sight to behold, this young football fanatic imagining he was Stanley Matthews bringing the crowd to their feet as he weaved his magic around ten empty bottles of Watney's Brown Ale without knocking any over.

In those far off days our football boots were not like the present-day lightweight models. Ours were very heavy, particularly if the pitch was rain sodden. In an effort to combat this problem I followed another tip I read which suggested trying to 'mould' your football boots to fit your feet so that they felt like one entity and lighter. So, I filled two large bowls with water, one cold and one hot. With boots firmly fixed on my feet I placed them alternatively into the two bowls. I'm sad to report it didn't do a scrap of good and I ended up waiting ages for the boots to dry out! It's tough training to be a star I can tell you.

None of this deterred me from my passion for the game. I became captain of my school team playing in, what was called in those days, the left half position. This is similar to today's midfield position. In those days, we didn't have the luxury of a dressing room to change in. We had to make do with a few pieces of corrugated iron sheets, the same as used for the Anderson Air Raid shelters. These sheets were interlocked and assembled into a tunnel long enough to provide room for 22 boys to change. There were no doors attached to either end and, by George, the wind didn't half blow through sometimes. Inside this structure, placed along each side, was a wooden bench seat for our clothes. On the occasions when we played a match on a muddy pitch, I couldn't get home quick enough to wash away the mud caked on my legs and arms. No luxury of baths and showers after a game for us budding stars.

Another memory I have is playing football on a pitch close to Wormwood Scrubs prison, with some of the inmates watching and shouting encouragement – at least that's what I think it was! – from their cell windows. If my memory serves me correctly, I think it was at the Scrubs, and also at Hackney Marshes, when we boys had to carry the goal posts to and from the pitch before and after each game. Another abiding memory for me was being selected to play for Middlesex Schoolboys in a big match against London Schoolboys. I can't recall the actual score; I think it was a draw. I was warned in advance to watch out for the boy playing centre forward for the Londoners, he was their star player and top goal scorer. So, I stuck next to him like a leech, wherever he went I followed. Whenever he got the ball I was there, tackling and worrying him so much that he ceased to pose any threat to us. At the finish I was congratulated for my performance, but that's enough of my self-glorification.

By now, around 1943, I had joined my brother David in becoming a member of the Boys' Brigade and we both played football for them. We won the league championship one year which meant we attended the annual Boys' Brigade get together at the Royal Albert Hall to receive our medals. The Royal Albert Hall is one of London's most distinctive and popular tourist attractions. The foundation stone of this unique building was laid by Queen Victoria in 1867 and named in memory of her beloved husband, Prince Albert, who had died six years earlier. The building was completed in 1871. During the Second World War it suffered little damage from the bombing raids. This could be because it is thought that many of the German planes used the unique structure of the building as a good landmark on their flight path! There are many entrances within the building enabling anyone to walk into the actual arena. Many of these entrances entail walking down a flight of carpeted stairways. Well, I can tell you from my experience that it wasn't easy walking down those steps wearing studded football boots and marching across the arena. Still, at least by this time my boots had dried out from the earlier (failed) bowls of water treatment.

I remember playing at the grounds of Walthamstow Avenue and Hendon. There were quite a few occasions when I played twice on a Saturday; the school team in the morning and the Boys' Brigade team in the afternoon. I remember my mother telling me one day not to play football because the day in question was Good Friday. She thought it wrong to play on such a day. She was quite right, as mothers usually are, because during the game I took the full force of a football, struck from close range, straight in the face, leaving me with a black eye. Talk about retribution for not listening to Mother! I still have my three medals earned from my footballing days, but not the black eye.

One of my school football team members was a very good friend of mine called Graeme Merton. He played in the right back position and was fairly tall and well built, which he used to his advantage, as many a recipient of his tackles would testify. His enthusiasm and the impact from his tackles led me to bestow upon him the accolade of 'Killer' Merton. When we were not playing football, we would travel from Park Royal tube station, on the Western Avenue not far from Hanger Lane, to London's Manor House station, near what is now called Haringey. This journey took us through 21 stops on the Piccadilly line. Upon arriving at Manor House, we would then fight our way onto a trolley bus to take us to White Hart Lane to see our favourite team, Spurs, play (me having changed my allegiance from Brentford and QPR to Tottenham). The big problem with this route was that when the game finished, there was always such a stampede to get on a trolley bus back to Manor House station. So, to avoid this near life-threatening mad rush, we would, reluctantly, leave about 10 minutes before the final whistle. As if that wasn't bad enough, there were occasions when, as we stood outside waiting for the bus to turn up, suddenly there would be a big roar from inside the stadium signifying a goal had been scored, but which team had scored was unknown to us until we got home. It was some years later when we found out we needn't have used that long arduous route to the ground at all. We found out we should have gone to Liverpool Street station where we could have caught a train direct to White Hart Lane! Still, I have happy memories of those days seeing players such as Ted Ditchburn, Alf Ramsey, Ronnie Burgess (the captain), Len Duquemin (from Guernsey) and Les Medley (who later in life emigrated to Canada), to name just a few. To illustrate the difference from those days to the present, I remember being on the bus to the ground one day and seeing Len Duquemin get off the bus when we reached White Hart Lane, carrying his football boots in a brown paper bag!

I never imagined in those days that one day, long into the future, I would not only walk onto Tottenham's actual playing pitch myself, but would also be sitting with my wife in the stands watching a son of mine playing on its hallowed turf! But this did actually happen in 2004 when our youngest son, Martin, aged 41 at the time, was playing for a team in a charity match. These charity matches were played at Tottenham's ground and amateur players were invited to apply for the chance of playing at White Hart Lane. Each team consisted of ten amateur players with the eleventh player, and captain, being a retired former Spurs player. Martin first played in one of these matches in 2003 when one of Tottenham's best strikers, Martin Chivers, was the team's captain. The following year, when my wife and I attended, Mickey Hazzard captained the team against a team with Ricky Villa in charge.

We were very proud to see our Martin run out onto the pitch and, despite the fact that he was whistled up once by the referee for a, shall we say, slightly over-enthusiastic tackle (bringing back memories of my friend Graeme) he acquitted himself very well, playing mainly a defensive role, but not afraid to undertake many forays into the opponent's half. I must add, he used both feet, but not at the same time, of course. I had a video camera that day and shot some footage which is always nice to revisit.

Before the game started, I was invited backstage where I saw the dressing rooms and hospitality areas which displayed many photographs and other memorabilia of many of the great players throughout the club's history. As if that wasn't enough, I was also allowed to walk out onto the pitch where I stood in one of the goal areas. It was something rather special for me as the memories came flooding back of standing on the terraces with

Graeme in those far off war-torn, austere, but also halcyon, days of my youth.

Around the time Graeme and I were attending matches together, footballers were on a maximum wage of £10-20 a week. It wasn't until 1961 when Fulham footballer Jimmy Hill won a battle with the Professional Footballers Association to scrap this maximum wage. This made headline news and Johnny Haynes, also a Fulham player, became the first player to get a wage of £100 per week. As I write this, footballers of the calibre of Len Duquemin earn around £200,000 a week! They certainly don't carry their own football boots around in a brown paper bag, either!

During the war years, many professional footballers were called up to one of the armed forces. This meant that many of those who became soldiers were posted to Aldershot, whereas Portsmouth was the natural base for sailors. The football clubs of these two towns were allowed to use any players posted there to play for them as guest players. This greatly increased their chances of winning, however, these matches were not the conventional league matches as these were suspended during the war years. Instead, regional league competitions were set up and played within the 50-mile travel limit the government had implemented during this time.

During this period, my father, after discussion with Mum, decided to take on a second job. This was as a turnstile operator at Wembley Stadium. During the war years there were some matches played at Wembley and

Dad was often able to obtain tickets for us. I saw England play Scotland once where English stars such as Frank Swift, Eddie Hapgood, Cliff Britton, Stan Cullis, Joe Mercer, Stanley Matthews, Raich Carter, Tommy Lawton, Jimmy Hagan, Jimmy Mullen, Leslie Smith and two of Scotland's finest, Matt Busby and Archie Macaulay, paraded their skills. After the war, there was a great interest in Speedway racing and, although I wasn't particularly interested in it, I did go to see it at Wembley a few times.

The Boys' Brigade

The Boys' Brigade movement was founded in 1883 by William Alexander Smith in Glasgow. It was his vision to bring young boys together with the aim of teaching them Christian values such as discipline, reverence, obedience, tolerance and comradeship. These were, and still are, similar aims to the Boy Scout Movement founded by Robert Baden Powell in 1908. From these humble beginnings the Boys' Brigade, usually referred to as the BB, grew to be a worldwide organisation involving millions of young people.

My eldest brother, Bert, had joined the BB before the outbreak of the Second World War, so we had some knowledge of the organisation. Apart from learning, absorbing, and practising the basic rules, Bert also used his innate musical talent to good effect by learning to play the bugle in the drum and bugle band. None of these activities appealed to my next brother Bernard, but as I have said earlier, it did interest the next in line, David, and subsequently, me. I joined as soon as

I reached the requisite age, which was 12 in those days. I must say it was a very wise move.

Although I was very fortunate in being the youngest of five children and raised in a happy, close-knit family unit, the BB gave me the opportunity and experience of going away on summer camps and mixing with likeminded boys, taking part in lots of sporting activities, learning new skills, having fun, standing on your own feet, or in other words, growing up.

Dave and I also learnt to play the bugle and joined the band. We were members of the West Middlesex Company based in Greenford which boasted a membership of 100 boys, the largest company in the world at that time. Another of the many benefits of being in the BB was learning the basic marching drills. This was a blessing when I later went into the RAF. Square bashing on the parade ground held no fears for me as I about-turned, formed fours and slow marched with consummate ease, all thanks to the BB.

Another blessing from my experiences in the BB of being away from home and mother's apron strings, enticing and loose as they were, was further brought home to me in the RAF when it is a somewhat sad revelation lying in bed in a billet and hearing some young conscript sobbing. This usually came from a boy who was an only child and had never been away from home before.

I remember my first summer camp. It was decided that we were all fit enough to cycle from Greenford to the village of Thame in Oxfordshire, a distance of 33 miles.

I only had a ladies' bike, which you can imagine brought forth a few ribald comments, but unphased, I made it both ways, as did everyone else. We camped in the grounds of a house belonging to a Colonel Birch Reynoldson, if my memory serves me right. There was a small swimming pool in the garden and as the weather was good, we took advantage of this nice facility. We also camped at Littlehampton in Sussex next to the seaside fairground and a new, just opened, pitch and putt golf course where, because by this time in my life I had started playing golf a little, I was invited to join the Mayor of Littlehampton for a game. Needless to say, he won. Well, the course was his brainchild in the first place so I couldn't show him up, could I?

Another summer camp I always remember started at Waterloo station on 15th August 1945. Whilst awaiting the train to take us to Lymington for the ferry trip across to Yarmouth on the Isle of Wight, we received the news that Japan had unconditionally surrendered, and the Second World War was finally over. As you can imagine, this news was greeted with great relief and unbounded happiness. We were determined that now we could relax and enjoy our holiday all the more, knowing that the last remaining dark clouds of six years of warfare would be replaced by the prospects and hopes of a bright new future for all.

On arrival at Yarmouth we were transported to our camp at Freshwater. Unfortunately, our euphoria wasn't to last – the expectant good weather didn't materialise and we had rain for about 10 days. It was so bad that our captain had no option other than to abandon the camp. Most of us returned home, leaving a couple of the officers aided by a number of the older members (my brother Dave being one) behind to dismantle the tents and generally clear the camp site before also leaving for home. Naturally, it was a big disappointment for all of us. The general opinion was that the town's name of Freshwater should be changed to Rainwater!

There was an incident at one of these summer camps, which one, I can't remember, but wherever it was, it made an impression on me which ultimately led to my first effort at writing. Because our company leader was a priest, we had a Sunday morning service and sometimes a church parade with our marching band in the afternoon. This service was held in a typical English field setting with the corn nearby gently waltzing to a warm summer breeze and the sound of bird song competing with the boys singing hymns, which naturally included the BB's anthem, *Will Your Anchor Hold in the Storms of Life?*

Singing whilst surveying the green lush, and now, thankfully, peaceful fields of our England, with the neat rows of our white bell tents and the big marquee where we had all our eagerly awaited meals, I was suddenly aware of how lucky I was to be free and surrounded by such warmth and camaraderie.

When the holiday finished, we returned home and back to school. It was usual for us to be given the task of writing an essay, or composition, as we called it in those days, about what we did on our summer holiday. I decided to try to describe the feelings I felt on that magical Sunday morning. My teacher was impressed with my humble effort and took it to the headmaster. He duly called me into his office and after congratulating me, asked me if I wanted to be a writer. To be honest, I didn't know what I wanted to be (other than a footballer). I replied that I had just tried to put into words the emotion I felt at that particular moment in time. Whilst I was pleased they liked my story, amateurish as it was, it was their reaction to it which brought home to me the power of words.

I learnt that the right words, even those in my amateurish story, can have the power to please, persuade, influence, comfort, inspire, move, disgust, console, anger and amuse – along with any other emotion you may think of. Their ability to stir our inner being is very evident in our wonderful and expressive English language. Speakers such as Winston Churchill, who wrote many wonderful phrases, and actors Laurence Olivier, John Gielgud and Richard Burton all knew how to use words to good effect. Similarly, so did musicians such as Cole Porter, who not only wrote his own music but also wonderful clever lyrics to accompany it. WS Gilbert (of Gilbert and Sullivan fame) and Noel Coward are others who also used their talent with words to amuse. Writers and poets also have this gift. Think of Shakespeare and the influence his use of words have had, and still do, on people the world over, similarly the words of Dylan Thomas and Oscar Wilde. Finally, we can't forget the work of the war poets, Wilfred Owen, Siegfried Sassoon, Rupert Brook, Robert Graves and John McCrea, who so brilliantly put the horrors of the First World War into such emotive and evocative words that are as powerful and poignant now as the day they were written.

This interest in words started for me from that summer camp awakening and led to my first effort at describing something I'd experienced by writing about it. This desire to write is something I find challenging, rewarding and satisfying (when I get it right!). I didn't study English to any great degree at my secondary school, so I have no illusions or pretensions about the quality of my efforts other than to say that I have been lucky in having quite a few articles published, some accompanied with photographs I've taken (photography being another passion of mine), so perhaps that says something! I enjoy trying to wax lyrical with poetry whether serious, light-hearted limericks, silly rhymes or just playing around with words. I think this love of writing is something inherent in our family. As many of you know, my father wrote his memoirs and my three brothers have also partaken, with varying success, in this pastime. I'm pleased to say both our sons have a penchant for words; Chris has a vivid, imaginative and humorous mind when writing stories, and Martin is very clear, analytical and persuasive with the written and spoken word. I just wish I had kept that original school composition but unfortunately, I didn't.

Another aspect of the Boys' Brigade which I enjoyed was marching through the streets playing my bugle on those Sunday church parades. Although, having said that, there was a downside to this. If the parade took place on a very hot summer's day, it is not easy to blow a bugle when you are dripping with perspiration and your lips keep slipping off the mouthpiece. Similarly, in complete contrast, it is also not easy to be woken up at some godforsaken hour from a deep sleep in your tent when it's your turn to blow reveille to wake up the rest of the camp.

Our company leader had decided that on our camp we should be segregated into groups in the same way some schools are into houses. Well, he decided that our contingent should be split into four groups, namely Eskimos, Hottentots, Mohawks and Zulus. I was a Zulu. In these days of political correctness, some people might take offence, thinking it degrading or trivialising these indigenous native people but, in those days, it was accepted, and bearing in mind the names used were suggested without any racial intent by our leader, a Church of England priest! Nevertheless, it could have had some repercussions arising from one particular Sunday church parade. We proudly marched through the streets, white sashes gleaming, cap badges, shoes shining and bugles firmly glued to our lips. The service went well and, as is usual at the end of any church service, when the final Amen is said, it is customary to have absolute silence for some seconds before anyone rises from their sitting or kneeling positions. Well, on this particular occasion, this respectful silence had only been observed for a few seconds when suddenly it was shattered by the sound of a lone young voice ringing through the rafters of this sacred and ancient building, inviting the congregation to join in the rallying cry of, "Up the Hottentots!" Fortunately, our leader thought it amusing, as did we boys. Billy Collins, the over-enthusiastic perpetrator, didn't though. Poor Billy, it was something he never lived down.

Chapter 6

Life After the War

The end of the war was celebrated throughout the country with street parties organised for the adults and children alike. We had one in Wedmore Road, and I remember the occasion well. Tables and chairs were arranged in the road outside our house which was conveniently situated equidistant from beginning and end of the road. There were Union Jacks proudly displayed everywhere and the feeling of utter joy and relief pervaded the whole atmosphere. The strain and worries from the six years of war seemed to be slightly lifted as the realisation and significance of this day gradually sank in.

There was one incident on that glorious day which I've always remembered. It happened when a soldier, a complete stranger, strolled down our road and not only joined us in our celebrations but also surprised us by singing a well-known popular song called *Together*. I like to think this is a song for anyone who's lost a loved one. It's about someone recalling good times past and gone, but not forgotten. The lyrics start by specifying particular things they enjoyed together and end in an uplifting manner by asserting that the memories of those times will remain everlasting.

We never did know who this soldier was or where he came from, but I can't help wondering if he was one of the many who had lost someone dear and found comfort, solace and strength in these heartfelt moving lyrics.

Britain After the War

After the euphoria of the war ending, the colossal task was one of coming to terms, for both victors and vanquished, with the terrible aftermath. The rebuilding of lives, cities, economics and infrastructures presented a formidable task requiring many years of hard work for all concerned. In Britain, we had a General Election in July 1945 and, despite all the efforts of the one man who led us to victory, Winston Churchill was not elected to carry on as Prime Minister. That job went to the leader of the Labour Party, Clement Attlee, a veteran from the First World War. Although Mr Attlee was small in stature and a mild, slightly insignificant-looking man, he had a firm resolve, deep conviction and determination to tackle the enormous task of picking up the pieces and trying to rebuild a new Britain.

Before that election, in May, there was a marvellous uplifting sight for all of us cricketing fans when an Australian team – made up of players just out of military service – came over and played five Test matches against England. This happy event was known as the Victory Tests, there were no Ashes involved, it was just a wonderful occasion for everyone to forget the war. One person who captured everyone's hearts was a dashing Australian named Keith Miller. He was an RAF fighter pilot, flying Mosquito aircraft in which he had survived quite a few narrow escapes. On the cricket pitch he was a revelation, a batsman who hit the ball with great ferocity to all corners of the ground. As well as that, he was a brilliant fielder and a top medium-to-fast bowler. There's a story saying that he once heard someone make a remark about the pressure of batting in a Test match, to which he is quoted as replying, "What pressure? I'll tell you what pressure is – pressure is having an enemy plane up your tail, that's pressure," although I believe he used a different word to 'tail'!

In 1946, Miller was joined by another Australian fast bowler, Ray Lindwall – who had a beautifully smooth bowling action – and the two of them together were the scourge of many an English batsman then and for many years after. I remember the Test match at Lords for two reasons. Firstly, I remember standing in the queue along with a pal of mine, also a cricket fan, while we eagerly awaited this cricketing spectacle. Secondly, as we were queuing, I remember seeing a giant poster advertising a new film, *Spellbound*. It struck me as memorable considering the magic of seeing Miller and Lindwall in action that day.

Directed by the master of suspense, Alfred Hitchcock, the film starred Gregory Peck and Ingrid Bergman. This is one of Hitchcock's top films and is still worth watching when it appears on television.

Rationing of food, clothing, confectionary (of vital importance to the children!) and many other items was to continue for years after the war. In January 1946, the first post-war consignment of bananas arrived in Britain. Many children had never seen a banana before.

Sadly, one little girl in Yorkshire died after eating four in a row, which had been given to her as a treat.

That's Entertainment

On a lighter note, hit songs of the period included *Cruising Down the River*, *We'll Gather Lilacs* and *A Gal in Calico* to name a few. Cinema audiences were queuing up to see *Brief Encounter* and *Blithe Spirit,* but my favourite was one called *State Fair.* This was a good old-fashioned, Americana, feel-good film. The music was by Rodgers and Hammerstein, and the best-remembered song from it was *It Might as Well be Spring.* The film starred Dana Andrews, singers Dick Haynes and Vivian Blaine, and a gorgeous girl named Jeanne Crain. The lush technicolor and full Hollywood make-up turned her into a goddess to us 14-year-old schoolboys. My sister used to read a film magazine called *Picturegoer* and one week its cover picture featured Jeanne Crain. Some of us boys wrote a letter to her requesting a signed photograph but, alas, no reply was received.

Some of the popular radio shows around this time were; *Dick Barton – Special Agent*; *Much Binding in the Marsh* – a comedy starring Kenneth Horne and Richard Murdoch as RAF officers on a RAF camp; *Stand Easy* – an Army-oriented comedy starring Cheerful Charlie Chester; *Water-logged Spa* – a navy comedy starring Eric Barker; and *Take it From Here* starring Jimmy Edwards, Dick Bentley and Kitty Bluett and, later, June Whitfield.

In the theatres, two big American shows hit London. The first was Irving Berlin's *Annie Get Your Gun,* followed by a show which changed the face of musical theatre, Rodgers and Hammerstein's *Oklahoma!*. The star of this show was a young, unknown to us baritone named Harold Keel, who subsequently changed his first name to Howard, went to Hollywood and the rest is history. Another show which also opened at this time was *Starlight Roof,* where a 12-year-old girl made a big impression with her singing. Her name? Julie Andrews.

Still Rolling!

By this time, my earlier interest in the cinema had continued to grow and I learnt a lot about the history and birth of the early days of silent movies, Charlie Chaplin, Buster Keaton, the Keystone Cops and the subsequent talkies. Fortunately, my friend Graeme also shared this interest, and we became frequent cinemagoers resulting in us becoming quite knowledgeable about films and the people who made them. This interest led to Graeme buying a cine camera and projector. Now fired with ambition, we decided to make our own movie. Another friend joined the 'cast' and between us we thought we'd try to make a gangster film. It was decided that as I could portray getting shot and dying the best, I would play the villain. We needed a scene where I walked into a large building, so off we went on location to a large block of flats along the Western Avenue. Dressed in a Humphrey Bogart/George Raft type raincoat with the collar turned up, and wearing a hat (borrowed from Graeme's dad) pulled down, I walked down the path and entered the doorway into the flats. Graeme thought he saw one or two enquiring faces peering down from their windows at this young 'film star' as he captured my actions on his camera using 9.5mm black and white film. All went well with that sequence, but after that we ran out of ideas. So, my big scene of being 'shot' never got recorded onto film, thus denying posterity the pleasure of seeing my Oscar-winning performance!

Later in 1946, a film came out called *The Jolson Story*, which was Hollywood's version of the life of singer Al Jolson. He was one of the biggest singing stars of the 1920s and '30s, appearing in vaudeville and Minstrel Shows. This entailed him blacking up his face and adopting a voice and accent similar to that heard in the deep south of America. In 1927, he made history by starring and singing in the world's first sound film, *The Jazz Singer*. During the Second World War he made frequent visits overseas to entertain the American troops. Hollywood's Warner Brothers and Columbia studios decided to make a film of this extraordinary entertainer's life but, by this time, Jolson was getting a little old and although his voice was still strong, the studio decided they wanted a younger man to take the part of Al Jolson. So, they brought in a lesser-known actor named Larry Parks. He could sing, but nothing like Jolson. So, it was decided that Larry Parks would sing along with recordings made by Jolson but by clever cutting, Parks's singing voice would be cut out. This method proved very successful and it was generally agreed that the end result was the best example of dubbing ever seen at that time. Graeme and I enjoyed the film and marvelled at the dubbing so much that we thought we would have a go. We bought an Al Jolson record, I blacked up my face with burnt cork, borrowed (again) a pair of white gloves from

Graeme's dad and performed and sang along to the record whilst Graeme filmed me. I must tell you that in those days our film was silent. So, once the film was developed, we would run it back through Graeme's projector onto a screen and, at the same time, play the original record of Jolson singing. Because the projector was a hand-operated machine, Graeme would try valiantly to keep turning the handle in synchronisation with the screen image of me opening and closing my mouth as I cavorted around, matching the sound of Jolson's voice booming out from the record. No easy feat I do assure you. Tragedy and laughter would sometimes happen when the film would get stuck in the gate of the projector. This jamming would freeze the screen image, but because the film couldn't move on it would overheat in the projector which manifested itself by producing a series of brown holes on the screen. As the heat intensified the holes got bigger and bigger before our very eyes. This forced Graeme to frantically turn the projector's handle faster and faster in a mad effort to free the affected jammed piece of film before the Fire Brigade were called. Whilst this fiasco was going on, the frozen screen image of me jumping around miming my head off (following the age-old tradition of 'the show must go on') was rapidly disappearing under the intense heat.

As well as being a good singer, Jolson would sometimes cup his white-gloved hands together and whistle a chorus or two during some of his songs. So, I thought I'd have a go, hence the borrowing of Graeme's dad's white gloves. As it turned out, that was one of our worst mistakes. During my frenzied attempts at whistling, I got some black marks from the burnt cork on my face onto the pristine white gloves! I bet they never had that trouble with *The Jolson Story*.

Although Graeme and I never made another film together, I did, later in life, acquire a camcorder to record family occasions and holidays, and by using two tape recorders and editing machines I produced VHS tapes combining images with music and narration for playing back through my VHS tape player, and not a white glove in sight.

Learning Music and Leaving School

When Dad, Bert and David were working at the Hazel Press, part of the building was rented out to a Mr Walter Phillips. He was a designer and marketed photographic mounts which were printed by the press for him. He told Dad that he liked his work and insisted on Dad doing his printing. He also told Dad that, one day, he intended to have his own printing press and would like Dad to come and work for him. His dream became reality in 1947 when the Walter Phillips Unicorn Press was opened in Perivale, and Dad left the Hazel Press and resumed his happy working relationship with Phillips by joining him at the Unicorn Press. This association lasted until Dad retired from the world of printing, a world in which he has left an indelible mark, in 1963, aged 70.

As mentioned earlier in my story, I am lucky to come from a musical family. My dad played piano and mandolin banjo and formed his own dance band during his time in Wales. Bert played tenor and alto saxophone, plus clarinet, and after the Second World War also formed his own dance band. My sister, Lily, also occasionally dabbled on the old Joanna (piano for the uninitiated). Bernard became interested in traditional jazz, learnt to play the trumpet and later joined the Greenford Rhythm Kings. David played bugle in the BB. As for me, I had some piano lessons from Dad when I was about 15 but my passion for sport was too powerful – I wanted to be out playing football, cricket, golf or tennis – so I stopped tinkling the ivories. It was a pity because I could pick out most of the popular melodies of the day using my right hand and I learnt a few chords for the left hand, but putting them together at the same time was not so easy. Dad and Mum were disappointed but, as usual, they accepted it was my decision and I can tell you it's a decision I have regretted ever since. I am green with envy when I see someone casually sit down at a piano and, without the need for any music, effortlessly play a tune. I could play the mouth organ and as previously mentioned, the bugle. Later on, Bert taught me to play the alto saxophone and eventually I became proficient enough to join forces with Bert. We spent many happy moments playing some of the old standards such as *Lover Come Back to Me, South of the Border*, and one of our all-time favourites, *If I Loved You* from Rodgers and Hammerstein's *Carousel*. I can still remember playing the lovely melody of this song on my alto sax and Bert coming in with the harmony line on his tenor. What wonderfully happy and treasured days they are. In the 1950s, I bought a guitar and joined the skiffle craze, but more about that later.

I also liked to sing and, although I don't profess to have a particularly good voice, it was enough to impress my teacher, so I was told. I would also sing for my Boys' Brigade tent mates on summer camps. Perhaps my love of singing and the ability to hold a tune comes from all that Welsh air I inhaled for the first four and a half years of my life?

I left school in 1946, aged 14, not knowing what I wanted to do except be a footballer. I was told that I had been watched by a scout from Brentford Football Club, but nothing came of that. Like my brother Bernard, I had no desire to go into the printing trade as it just didn't appeal to me. I'd quite enjoyed my school days, I liked sport, reading, writing, geography, history and singing. My maths, or arithmetic as it was called in those days, was alright, but I never could make head nor tail of logarithms or algebra.

So, not knowing what to do, I spent a few weeks hanging around at home until one day my dad heard of a vacancy in a local factory which made tables and chairs. Dad and I took a bus to this emporium of wood, which was situated in Southall, to meet the manager. To be truthful I wasn't really interested in the job – I'd have much preferred if the factory were making goalposts or flag posts for football pitches rather than tables and chairs – but the pressure was on and I had no choice other than to accept the job offer.

The job entailed me standing at a bench which had a vice fixed firmly to it. On one side of the bench, neatly stacked, was a pile of table legs. After picking up a leg, I would insert it into the vice which I would then tighten. The next operation was to pull down a handle, which had a drill attached to it, and drill a hole into the table leg. Then I'd loosen the vice, remove the leg (now complete with a beautifully cut clean hole) and place it with pride in a pile of similar 'holey' legs on the other side of the bench. Then I would return to the 'unholey' mountain of legs and repeat this tricky operation. I felt like a sort of human woodworm! For this task, I was paid the princely sum of £1.30 a week. No wonder there was a vacancy for the job.

After two weeks of this, I decided that I didn't want to be lumbered with the world of wood anymore, so I gave in my notice and decided to leg it. Naturally, Mum and Dad were disappointed but accepted that it wasn't for me. I had a few weeks of convalescence at home until Mum took the initiative and told me she had found me another job. No bus trip was required for this new venture because the job was in a shoe repair shop just around the corner from home. Off I went, leaving the world of wood behind and entered one of leather.

Much to my surprise, I found the job quite interesting. There is a sense of achievement in removing the worn-out soles and heels of a pair of shoes and replacing them with new leather, which, after polishing, made them look as good as new. The shop was owned and run by a husband and wife who were not only very pleasant and kind to me, but also increased my pay to £2 a week. I settled into this job well, learning the noble art of cobbling. I stayed there for a couple of years and then moved to another cobbler's shop for more money and lasted there until I was 18 and called up for National Service. Even then I carried on pounding and polishing leather, except that by this time it was more on boots than shoes.

Disaster and Luck

Disaster struck our family in 1947 when Mum was ill and after many hospital visits was diagnosed with cancer. An operation was scheduled for January 1948. My brother, Bernard, who was now in the army in Palestine, was allowed home on compassionate leave. The operation was successful and Mum came home. Two of Dad's sisters came and stayed with us, helping with the nursing for Mum. After about a month, Bernard's compassionate leave ended and he was sent back to Palestine. He was very lucky when a train he was travelling on through Gaza was blown up by a Jewish terrorist organisation, as 13 servicemen were killed and many more seriously injured, but Bernard escaped with only minor injuries.

Sadly, in May 1948, Mum suffered a relapse and went back into hospital for another operation. The news was so bad that the surgeon warned us to prepare for the worst. Once more Bernard was flown home on compassionate leave. It was certainly a dark and worrying time for our family. I remember lying in bed one night thinking deeply about the situation and praying, when suddenly I had what I can only describe as a warm glow enveloping me and telling me that everything was going to be alright, and that Mum would recover. It was a little uncanny but the feeling was so strong that I told my brother Dave about it. Whether it was divine intervention, a miracle or just luck, I don't know, but what I do know is that, thankfully, due in no small measure to the nursing care she received from Dad's two sisters, Mum made a fantastic recovery and we were blessed in having her with us for a few more years.

Chapter 7

The End of the Decade

Great British Weather

Rewinding back to the year 1947, we saw some severe weather throughout the country. We had some snow before Christmas 1946 but it was on 21st January 1947 when it really started. This was to be one of the worst winters the UK has ever had. From Scotland to Devon the country was blanketed in snow. All forms of transport were badly affected, including food deliveries and coal supplies, which resulted in some power stations closing. Electricity supplies to homes was reduced to 19 hours per day. To add to the misery, bitter winds blew and temperatures plummeted. Helicopters dropped food supplies for people in many cut off villages, particularly in Devon, and the armed forces were deployed to keep roads and rail tracks clear. Of course, in those days, most houses didn't have central heating or double-glazed windows. Most heating was from coal fires – provided coal was available – and this meant that once you left a coal-heated room the rest of the house was bitterly cold. Going to the toilet necessitated a mad dash upstairs and then back again to the warmth of the sitting room. Similarly, going to bed required extra blankets and getting up each morning for work was most unpleasant.

The bad weather conditions were compounded by the worrying economic situation with Britain and Europe suffering severe shortages of essential goods. But once again America came to the rescue, this time with the Marshall Plan. This was a huge financial package named after American General George Marshall who, on a visit to Europe in 1947, saw how bad the infrastructure of Britain was and how much of Western Europe had suffered from the war. The Marshall Plan was instigated with the aim of aiding Europe by supplying food and the other vital supplies necessary in a humanitarian crusade of recovery from the war.

As well as the terrible winter weather of 1947, two years after the war Britain was still a country of rationing and austerity. Whenever word got out that some particular shop had just taken delivery of a rarely seen food item, mothers would rush with their shopping bags and ration books to stand stoically in the queue hoping to be lucky.

Onwards and Upwards

After the 1936 Berlin Olympic Games had finished, the next games, scheduled for 1940, should have taken place in Tokyo but, due to political reasons, Japan declined and Helsinki was substituted. Unfortunately, the advent of the Second World War intervened, and no games took place until 1948. London was the chosen venue for their return. Due to the war, Germany and Japan were banned from entering and Russia declined the invitation, but despite of this there were still over 4,000 competitors – of which there were only 355 women – representing 59 nations. The availability of food and accommodation were, if anything, worse than during the war. Britain's athletes trained at Butlins holiday camps and many RAF stations provided accommodation for the athletes.

Despite all the austerity and lack of resources, Britain pulled out all the stops and the games were a triumph and a heart-warming tribute to the sheer determination and hard work of the organisers and participants. The final medal table showed that Britain finished in 12th place by winning an overall total of 23 medals: three gold, 14 silver and six bronze. I remember seeing King George VI and Queen Elizabeth II opening the games (I even remember John Mark, the final athlete who had the honour of carrying the torch into Wembley Stadium and igniting the Olympic flame). The athletics and field events took place in the Stadium, the Empire Pool in Wembley hosted the swimming events, rowing was at Henley-on-Thames and sailing at Torbay in Devon. The estimated total cost was around £732,000, quite a difference from the £11billion cost when the games returned to London in 2012!

At this time, of course, colour television hadn't arrived, but even in black and white it was still a thrill to see the world's best athletes competing in this magnificent sporting spectacle. Two people I remember are McDonald Bailey, a fine sprinter from Trinidad, and a remarkable lady from Holland with the equally remarkable name of Fanny Blankers Koen. This lady or 'The Flying Dutchwoman' as some wits called her, dominated the ladies' track events by winning four gold medals – the 100m, 200m, 80m hurdles and the 100m relay – which was certainly not bad for a 30-year-old mother of two.

Events of the Late 1940s

Some respite from the harsh winter weather conditions of the late 1940s eventually came when summer arrived. There was a complete change in the weather with sunny days and temperatures soaring above 30 degrees centigrade in June 1947.

When the cricket season got under way there was one man in particular who will never be forgotten. His name was Denis Compton. He was a dashing, daring, devil-may-care batsman who went into the history books by scoring 18 centuries and amassing 3,816 runs in the 1947 season. He was also an unorthodox left arm spin bowler. He brought a wave of fresh air with his new style of cricket by dashing down the wicket and sweeping or cutting the ball to all four corners of the ground, much to the delight of the spectators. He formed a fantastic partnership with Bill Edrich in the Middlesex team, as well as for England. His face was seen on posters around the country because, due to his dark good looks, he was used to advertise the hair product Brylcream. Denis Compton, along with his brother Leslie, was also an accomplished footballer playing for Arsenal as a left winger. He played for England in some wartime international games and, in 1950, won a medal playing in the Cup Final when Arsenal beat Liverpool. Compton joined the army during the Second World War and was posted to India. He died in 1997 aged 78. His great partner Bill Edrich may not have had the dashing flair of Compton when batting, but he was also a batsman of outstanding ability and his partnership with Compton was one of the most successful of all time. Edrich was a fighter – not only on the cricket field but also during the Second World War when, serving as an RAF Bomber Pilot,

Squadron Leader Edrich was awarded a DFC. He, like his great partner Compton, also played football, turning out for Norfolk and later Spurs. Squadron Leader WJ Edrich DFC died in 1986 aged 70. In memory of one of the best partnerships to ever grace the cricket scene, two stands – the Denis Compton and the Bill Edrich stands – were erected side by side at the Nursery End of Lords Cricket Ground, which is a truly fitting tribute to these two giants who brought so much pleasure to cricket fans.

The year 1947 is also memorable as it was the year when the Labour government's minister, Aneurin Bevan, finally saw his dream realised when the National Health Service, which would provide free medical treatment to all citizens of Britain, was introduced. This public health service has been the envy of the world ever since.

There was widespread interest and joy throughout the country on 20th November 1947, when 21-year-old Princess Elizabeth married Prince Philip in Westminster Abbey. This happy event was watched by 2,000 invited guests in the Abbey and broadcast to 200 million people around the world. The newlyweds honeymooned at Birkhall on the Balmoral Estate in Scotland.

The year 1949 bought the end of clothes rationing which had been imposed in 1941. The ban on coloured lights, floodlights and neon signs was also lifted, but the most popular change, with children at least, was the end of confectionary rationing. I also remember the Wimbledon Tennis Championship coming alive that year when an American lady named Augusta (Gussie) Moran shocked the old brigade and caused a near riot amongst the court side press photographers with her lace-trimmed knickers peeping out beneath her white dress. Designed by Teddy Tinling, her daring outfit resulted in her being asked to open garden fetes, beauty contests and even hospitals. I believe she had a racehorse named after her, too! She wasn't exactly one of the top tennis players as such, but I think we can say that she was a smash hit who taught us to love all, which served to her advantage by winning the game, set and match!

The world's first jet airliner, the De Havilland Comet, made its first flight test in July 1949 at Hatfield, Hertfordshire, when pilot Group Captain John (Cat's Eyes) Cunningham took the plane up. In September that year another first flight occurred when what was considered to be the world's biggest aeroplane, the Bristol Brabazon, at 130 tons and powered by eight Rolls-Royce engines with a carrying capacity of 100 passengers, frightened the life out of many birds when she took to the skies. The interior of the plane proudly displayed a cinema, cocktail bar, a lounge and dining room, sleeper berths and separate men's and ladies' dressing rooms. Despite it flying for some time, due to the sheer cost of travelling on it allied with much political intrigue and shenanigans, it was deemed to be a white elephant and not a commercially viable proposition, so, in 1953, it was scrapped.

In complete contrast, at about the same time as the Brabazon flights – or maybe it was because of them? – a flock of starlings decided to have a meeting on the minute hand of Big Ben. This caused the clock to lose four and a half minutes; it's slowest in 90 years.

Disaster struck in September when the economic situation worsened and more belt-tightening was required. Sugar supplies were cut to 8oz per person per week. Milk and tobacco supplies were also cut and, much to the dismay of us children, confectionary was back on ration at 4oz per person per week.

Tommy Handley, the Liverpudlian comedian, who did so much to raise the morale of the British people during the Second World War with his Thursday night radio show *ITMA*, died aged 56 on 9th January 1949 from a brain haemorrhage. The BBC first launched this show for a trial run of four episodes in July 1939. As the months went by and the daily news became full of Adolf Hitler's march across Europe, the press began referring to Hitler as, It's that man again. The BBC decided to use the Hitler phrase in its abbreviated form *ITMA* as the title for the show, but this time the man in question wasn't Hitler, but someone who brought laughter and hope to the whole nation during its darkest hour. In 1941, the whole cast were invited to perform a special edition at Windsor Castle to celebrate Princess Elizabeth's 16th birthday. Some of the regular cast members included Maurice Denham, Jack Train, Deryck Gulyer and Hattie Jacques.

To illustrate the huge debt the people owed Tommy Handley and the high esteem in which he was held, on the day of his funeral it is estimated that along the six-mile route from the private Chapel in Westbourne Grove in London to Golders Green, thousands mourned his passing. In addition, memorial services were carried out in St Paul's Cathedral and in Tommy's home city at Liverpool Cathedral.

The final years of the 1940s saw the coal industry nationalised in 1947, followed by the railways in 1948. This year also went into our history books with the advent of mass immigration into Britain when around

500 people from the West Indies travelled from Jamaica aboard the SS Empire Windrush and arrived at Tilbury Docks. This was an historic event which took a long time for all the involved parties, immigrants and the British, to adjust to and accept the different attitudes and cultures, including to say nothing of the weather which was vastly different from Jamaica. Eventually, it worked out, and with housing and work prospects being readily available, it wasn't long before others made their exodus from their Caribbean homes seeking a new life in Britain.

There is no doubt that with Britain still in disarray and turmoil from the war, the extra labour force they provided along with their positive attitude was a very welcome aid which eventually broke down any prejudices felt by some. Those early pioneers from the SS Windrush could never have envisaged the impact their 1948 journey would have, and I imagine would be amazed if they could see the integration and multi-racial Britain of today.

Home and Away, and a Narrow Escape

My brother Bernard was demobbed from the army in 1948 and returned to Civvy Street. By this time, he was married to Joan, a lovely local girl, and the proud father of a baby girl who they named Valerie. He decided he wanted to become a quantity surveyor and accepted a post with a London building company as a trainee. By studying hard and attending night school three nights a week, he achieved his aim and became a fully qualified member of that esteemed fraternity.

The next year, 1949, saw my next brother David being called up for his National Service. Like Dad, Bert, Bernard and my sister Lily, he joined the khaki brigade and was put into the Royal Corps of Signals and hated every minute of his 18 months' National Service.

I was still an avid film buff and sportsman. My good friend Graeme and I played golf on a nine hole course at nearby Perivale Park, and I must admit it brought back memories of earlier days when I and a few other boys in our gang, including my brother Dave, would hide amongst the trees on many a morning looking for 'lost' golf balls, and then try to sell them to approaching golfers on the course with the sole aim of gaining enough money to go swimming in the afternoon. As the wonderful television character Arthur Daley would later say about such an enterprise, it was a nice little earner! Similarly, on the sporting scene, Graeme and I would spend Sunday afternoons playing 18 holes on a public putting course, followed by an hour or two on the tennis court.

Talking of Graeme, I also remember with affection his mother, Avis Merton, who was a professional actor and very much involved in the local theatre group. I remember how well she played the lead part of the teacher Miss Moffatt in the well-known play *The Corn is Green* by Emlyn Williams. The company also performed Gilbert and Sullivan operettas and she often tried to persuade the two of us to join the group. We thought about asking *Princess Ida* and *Iolanthe* to come with us but were frightened we might have *The Yeomen of the Guard* after us which could end up with us two facing a *Trial by Jury* thus making our *Utopia, Limited*. So, after much deliberation, we eventually agreed that we didn't have the patience or desire to join *The Pirates of Penzance* or *The Gondoliers* on *HMS Pinafore*, and politely declined his mother's overtures.

Part 3
1950s

Chapter 8

New Beginnings

For some people, the 1950s in Britain were dull and grey, but for others it was the start of a new beginning. For me personally, looking back in subsequent years I realised the fifties were my defining years.

We were still recovering from the war years. Austerity, rationing and bombsites – some of which still had hidden UXBs (unexploded bombs) buried deep within the rubble – were still part of daily life. There were plenty of old air raid shelters still in evidence and concrete hexagonal look out shelters strategically placed around the country, from which soldiers or Home Guardsmen would watch through narrow slits along each side of the shelter for any enemy parachutists. As I write this the year is 2021, and I can tell you that there are many of these concrete structures still standing throughout the UK, minus the guardians inside, of course.

Turn of the Decade

These were the days when authority was respected. Adults would reprimand any unruly children, whether their own or someone else's, without the fear of arrest or reprisals. This meant that children grew up instilled with the discipline of acceptance and not questioning their elders. In a strange way it gave the children a sense of understanding and security. Television in 1950 was still a luxury with fewer than two million sets sold in Britain. Many considered the 'box' in the corner of the room to be a threat to family life. Of course, the pictures were black and white, there were no daytime programmes and the service closed at 11pm every night. In addition, there was a one-hour break in transmission every evening between five and six o'clock. This was named the 'toddlers' truce'. Small children, believing that television was closing down for the night, a belief instilled in them by their tired parents, were packed off to bed. This parent-friendly ploy by the BBC lasted until 1957.

In May 1950, petrol rationing finally ended after 10 years. People were tearing up their petrol rationing books and dancing around their cars. The Whitsun weekend of wonderful weather saw thousands take to the roads in celebration. The next month, in typical government fashion, they put up the price of petrol to three shillings a gallon.

The first self-service shop in Britain opened in Croydon, south London in June 1950, meaning shopping without waiting in line to be served. Part of the aftermath of the war was a shortage of labour, but fortunately this problem was greatly eased by the thousands of immigrants from the Commonwealth countries, particularly from the West Indies, who had been coming over since 1948. By the mid-1950s, figures showed up to 3,000 people per month were arriving, seeking work and a new life in the UK.

Sadly, there were some famous people who died in 1950. This included authors Eric Blair, better known as George Orwell, the writer of *1984* and *Animal Farm*, and George Bernard Shaw, whose book *Pygmalion* inspired the musical *My Fair Lady*. At least Shaw took the advice of Scottish singer and comedian Sir Harry Lauder who advocated everyone 'keep right on to the end of the road', and lived to 94. Unfortunately, Sir Harry couldn't heed his own advice, and died aged 77.

On the sporting scene we saw American Budge Patty win the men's single title at Wimbledon, whilst fellow American Louise Brough took the Ladies' Trophy for the third year running. Arsenal won the FA Cup. The golf Open Championship was won by South African Bobby Locke for the second year running. The Grand National was won by Freebooter and the Derby saw a horse named Galcador first past the post.

Whilst there were many popular films being released, such as *All About Eve*, *Sunset Boulevard* and *King Solomon's Mines*, radio was still king in most homes with favourites like *Variety Bandbox*, *Dick Barton – Special Agent* and *Life with the Lyons* (this programme starred Americans Bede Daniels, her husband Ben Lyon and their two children Barbara and Richard). Bede and Ben had endeared themselves to the British public during the Second World War by not rushing back to the luxury and safety of their American home, instead choosing to stay in London throughout the frightening days of the Blitz and putting out a weekly comedy radio programme called *Hi Gang,* which did a lot to raise morale.

King George VI opened the restored House of Commons, which had been destroyed in an air raid in 1941. Whilst on a completely different plane, three generations of the Bowler family attended a celebration to mark the centenary of the Bowler hat.

The BBC transmitted TV pictures live across the Channel from France for the first time on 27th August, when a two-hour programme was sent from Calais to Dover and relayed on to London. There was only a single, two-second break during the whole transmission and reception was reported to have been very good.

In 1951, another record was set when Britain's first jet bomber, the Canberra, crossed the Atlantic to Canada in a time of four hours and 40 minutes. While in Scotland, the Stone of Scone which had gone 'missing' from Westminster Abbey, was found in an abandoned Abbey near Forfar, Arbroath, after a 107-day search.

The big event of the year, however, was the Festival of Britain. This was held to mark the centenary of the Great Exhibition of 1851. London was of course the main focal point, but it was also celebrated, albeit in a much smaller way, throughout the country. Although the King was unwell at the time, he still attended the opening ceremony on 4th May. Despite the austerity, which still existed in Britain, the event was a showpiece for British industry, art and design. It also raised the spirits of the people and gave them hope for a brighter future. Twenty-seven acres of derelict, bomb-weary, scarred land on London's South Bank was transformed for the exhibition. There was a Dome of Discovery, and floating and floodlit above all of this like an exclamation mark, was the aluminium Skylon. This structure had no visible means of support, which prompted one wryly observe that it symbolised Britain at that time.

By the time the festival closed in September, figures show that around eight and half million people had visited this innovative morale-boosting spectacle. One building, The Royal Festival Hall, was designated as the only permanent structure and even today it still serves as a very popular venue for many entertaining functions. As well as working right next door to it for many years afterwards, I also visited it many times, including once when I snuck in without a ticket – they were sold out and it was the only way I could get in to see the Chris Barber Jazz Band with special guest, American Blues and Folk Singer, Big Bill Broonzy (that's another story!). Down river at Battersea Park, a kaleidoscope of colour in the guise of a giant fun fair was awaiting the thousands who flocked there to forget the years of austerity and rationing for a few hours and enjoy a breath of fresh air, laughter and freedom.

The General Election in October 1951 saw the youngest ever Tory candidate enter the contest. Her name was Margaret Roberts, who later made a bit of a name for herself as Margaret Thatcher, and later, Lady Thatcher.

This election also marked the return to power of Winston Churchill as Prime Minister.

Another big event which occurred in October 1951 was when Princess Elizabeth and Prince Philip undertook a tour of Canada on behalf of her father, King George VI, who was too ill to travel. The Princess and Prince flew to Montreal and embarked on their tour, taking in around 60 cities and towns, travelling by train, aircraft and even naval vessels. Everywhere they went they were greeted by vast welcoming crowds.

The UK received quite a shock in 1951 when it was announced that two Foreign Office diplomats, Guy Burgess and Donald Maclean, who had been under surveillance by the Intelligence Services as suspected spies, got wind of the surveillance and fled to Soviet Russia. Meeting at Cambridge University some years earlier, along with Kim Philby, they were all deeply involved in espionage, holding very left-wing views of western democracy and passing secrets to the Russians.

The year 1951 also saw the Peak District being designated as Britain's first National Park. This was followed in the same year by the Lake District and Snowdon receiving National Park status. The man who brought Radar – radio, detection and ranging – to the world, Sir Robert Watson-Watt, was, quite rightly, awarded £50,000 in 1951 by a grateful government. The whole world owes a massive debt to this Scotsman.

This was also the year the government abolished Identity Cards which, for security reasons, had been introduced at the outbreak of the war in 1939. Cheese rationing was cut to 1oz per person per week, but tea rationing ended – much to the delight of the whole nation. On 5th July, central London's last tram made its final journey from Woolwich to New Cross. I remember as a small boy being taken on the trams by my parents when visiting my mother's sister and family in Peckham. It was a novelty for me and my siblings to ride on this noisy but reliable mode of transport.

A shock came when the then Chancellor of the Exchequer, Hugh Gaitskill, announced there would be a prescription charge for dentures and spectacles. This charge, which was in contradiction of the National Health pledge of free medical treatment, was said to be due to the financial demands relevant at the time. This surprise act upset Aneurin Bevan (the man who introduced the National Health Service in 1948) so much that he resigned his post as Minister of Labour in protest.

Meanwhile in London's West End, Agatha Christie's play *The Mousetrap* starring husband and wife Richard Attenborough and Sheila Sim opened at the Ambassadors Theatre on 25th November 1951. It switched to St Martin's Theatre in 1974. Now, in 2022, over 70 years later, it is still running at St Martin's Theatre in London, but obviously not with the same actors and certainly not with the same cheese!

1952 started with a shock when, on 6th February, King George VI died peacefully in his sleep. Princess Elizabeth and Prince Philip quickly returned from their holiday in

Kenya. The much-loved King, who reluctantly became King when his brother King Edward VIII abdicated in 1936, and was King throughout the Second World War, died from lung cancer aged 56. His body lay in state in Westminster Hall where thousands of the general public paid their respects. He was buried on 15th February in St George's Chapel, Windsor Castle.

The latter part of 1952 bought a series of disasters in Britain. In August, the people of Devon suffered when heavy rain broke the banks of East and West Lyn rivers. The flood water hit the resort of Lynmouth, killing 36 people and forcing many others to leave their homes. The next month another tragedy struck when 28 spectators died when a prototype jet plane crashed at the Farnborough Air Show. As if that wasn't enough, in October, 102 people died as a Perth to London express and a northbound train from Euston crashed into a stationary commuter train at Harrow and Wealdstone station. Finally, in December we were subjected to dense fog which enveloped London. This 'smog', as it was called, only lasted a few days but it was estimated that its poisonous fumes indirectly killed around 4,000 people, particularly the elderly.

Chapter 9

National Service

Joining the RAF

As the youngest member of the family, I grew up listening to stories about army life from my father, three brothers and my sister. So, when I reached my 18th birthday in December 1949, I was required to serve my 18 months of National Service. For this I was instructed to attend an interview whereby questions were asked to ascertain which arm of the services I might be suitable for. Fortunately, remembering what I'd heard about army life from my family members, I applied to join the Royal Air Force. My request was granted and, in March 1950, a letter arrived from our friendly government, inviting me to report to the RAF camp at Padgate in Lancashire on 28th March, and so began my National Service with the RAF.

One of the first things to do upon arrival at Padgate was for all of us to get kitted out with uniforms and a myriad number of other items deemed essential to make Airmen out of us fresh-faced and slightly bemused 'erks' – the nickname for all such young and inexperienced newcomers. What followed next was, for me, quite hilarious. We were marched to a store hut in which a group of NCOs (non-commissioned officers) were standing behind counters, awaiting our arrival. The first item of kit was thrust into our arms with great rapidity as we were hurried along the counters to collect the rest of our kit. Boots, shoes, underclothes, socks, shirts, collars, ties, sweaters, trousers, battledress tunics and 'best blue' uniforms. Two hats, one a beret and the other a forage cap, woollen gloves and the very necessary item for the time of year, our greatcoat, completed the list. Next came polishing equipment for cleaning all the uniform brasses, boots and shoes, a drinking mug, cutlery, knife, fork and spoon (referred to as 'irons') and other items deemed necessary by the powers that be. All of these items came flying through the air at great speed accompanied by shouts from the NCOs to, "Hurry up chaps!" (or words to that effect). The sight of all these 'sprogs' (another nickname for newcomers) with boots and shoes tied around their necks, their faces lost behind all the other equipment gathered in their arms, blindly staggering around the room, crashing into each other and wondering what on earth had hit them was just too much for my goonish sense of humour. I was doubled up with laughter! Of course, with such loads precariously balanced it was inevitable that some items would fall to the ground causing the unfortunate sprog, panic-stricken by now, to struggle to redeem their fallen articles. Their clumsiness bought more verbal encouragement from the NCOs and more laughter from me.

All of this paraphernalia required a large kitbag to carry it, which was another entertaining fiasco. Each individual kitbag required some form of identity, so we were all given stencilling equipment and instructions on how to stencil our service number onto the bag, and underneath the number, the current month followed by a hyphen then the last two numbers of the current year. In our case, as it was March 1950, the finished version should show our service number with 3-50 underneath. Now, in an effort for absolute clarity, the Corporal said, and I quote this verbatim, "Put three hyphen 50 – five zero." Simple enough really, but of course there's always one isn't there? This poor embarrassed lad took the instruction literally and his kitbag ended up showing his serial number and underneath the numbers 3-50 50. As you can imagine, the Corporal was less than delighted, whilst the rest of us thought it hilarious.

Equally funny was marching back to our billets after being issued with rifles and tin helmets. These helmets were supposed to stay on your head but some lads had great difficulty in achieving this, despite inclining their heads alarmingly far to one side. Failure to master this technique resulted in the helmet leaving the head and landing in the road with an almighty clatter. As the unfortunate lad tried to retrieve it, the marching feet of his colleagues kicked it as they tried their best not to fall over it. We all learnt a few new words that day I can tell you.

After Padgate I was posted to RAF Wilmslow in Cheshire for eight weeks' square-bashing. In those days, there were about 2,000 WAAFs (Women's Auxiliary Air Force) stationed there, but what with the sheer physical hard work (not to mention the bromide in the tea) we were too exhausted to chase after them!

Another incident which caused much merriment occurred whilst the platoon was drilling on the parade ground. The Drill Sergeant bellowed out the command, "About turn" and we all 'about turned' – all except one silly devil who blindly continued marching straight on all on his own. This prompted the Drill Sergeant to break into song and the first five notes and words of *Beautiful Dreamer, Wake unto Me* wafted across the parade ground. I have often wondered if that particular dreamer was the same man with the iconic 3-50 50 on his kitbag!

It was during those drill moments on the parade ground that I was grateful for my days in the Boys' Brigade. Marching, including slow marching, forming fours, about turning etc. were all drill movements I had learnt from the age of 12. The RAF taught me to use rifles and Sten guns. I managed to gain the accolade of being a marksman in rifle shooting. I knew watching all those rooting, tooting, fast-shooting cowboy films in my youth would come in handy one day.

After I had completed six of the normal eight weeks' square bashing, I contracted, for the second time, scarlet fever and was put in the isolation ward of the camp hospital for two weeks of treatment. Afterwards, I was sent home for two weeks' convalescence before returning to camp for the passing out parade signifying my square-bashing time at RAF Wilmslow was over.

Unfortunately, in June 1950 the Korean War broke out, resulting in the government increasing the required National Service time from 18 months to two years for all current and future conscripts. I have good reason for remembering this because, by this time, I was stationed at No.3 Radio School, Compton Basset in Wiltshire, undergoing training as a teleprinter operator. There were rumours going around that our class was earmarked for Korea, but luckily for us we were let off and destined to stay in the UK. So, the extra six months' service in the UK was accepted and infinitely preferable to being shot at in Korea. This war became known as the 'The Forgotten War' because whenever people are discussing past wars and conflicts you can bet your life that the Korean War is usually not mentioned.

As a matter of interest, from the end of the Second World War in August 1945 (not May 1945 – that was when the war in Europe finished) to the end of National Service conscription in 1960, there were about 400 national servicemen killed in action, plus many more wounded in conflicts in Malaysia, Kenya, Cyprus, Suez Canal, Aden, the Gulf States and Korea.

Compton Basset

When our teleprinter training started at Compton Bassett, the first thing we had to learn was how to not only type but become a touch typist. We did this on a manual typewriter with the aid of a record which provided a rhythmic beat to which we endeavoured to hit the right keys in unison. As any typist knows, there are certain phrases which are used as typing exercises for learners. Phrases such as, Now is the time for all good men to come to the aid of the party, probably being the best well-known. Another one, which is less known, used all the letters of the alphabet (a pangram), A quick movement of the enemy will jeopardize six gunboats. Easy you might think, but just imagine this scenario. You're a total novice typist, trying like mad to keep in time with the beat emanating from the old shellac 78rpm record, when the classroom door opens and your commanding officer enters with his subordinates in tow. This unexpected intrusion by the top brass was too much for one nervous young lad. He was concentrating manfully when, suddenly, he became aware of the top brass standing right behind him, breathing down his neck, resulting in him typing the letter I instead of U in the last word of the pangram, thereby changing it to, A quick movement of the enemy will jeopardize six ginboats. Fortunately, the commanding officer moved swiftly on, probably for a quick G and T themselves, and the red-faced lad survived.

As the camp at Compton Bassett was only about 85 miles from my Greenford home, I tried sneaking off on a Friday evening and hitch-hiking home. The first time a friend and I tried it, the first lift we got was on an open top lorry where we froze for about an hour before we were turfed off. The next lift entailed both of us sitting in the driver's cab of a stinking diesel lorry for most of the night. There were frequent stops allowing the driver to have forty winks. The journey took all night and when I finally arrived home, I went straight to bed to recover from this motoring nightmare.

Another method for getting home was to take the official coach that left from the camp Guardhouse to London every Saturday lunchtime and left King's Cross on Sunday evening for the return trip. This comfortable alternative was organised by a flight sergeant by the name of Field, in conjunction with a local coach company named Cards of Devizes, and cost 18 shillings return. This seemed a good idea, the only snag was that we had to wait until Saturday lunchtime before we could head for home. So, a third option was sought and found. This third option was a retrograde step-in that entailed the dreaded hitch-hiking home on a Friday evening and travelling back by the midnight train from Paddington to Swindon on Sunday night. The journey took two hours and on arrival at Swindon there were various coaches waiting to collect and transfer the Airmen back to one of the many RAF camps in Wiltshire at that time. As none of the waiting coaches went direct to Compton Bassett, we were told by those who knew better to board a coach destined for the camp at Yatesbury, which was a mere 3-4 miles from Compton, and upon arrival at Yatesbury we were to mingle with the Yatesbury lads as they left the coach for their billets, and then we would calmly walk out of the camp's main gate and head off to walk the 3-4 miles to Compton Bassett. This was fine in theory, but on the first night that we tried this ploy the coach driver spotted us making towards the main gate and in his broad West Country accent shouted out to us, "Where be you'n going then?" When we said Compton Bassett, he went mad replying, "What you'n doin' on my coach, this be for the Yatesbury lads, bloody cheek, bloody Comp'on Bass-it blokes, you'n got no right bein' yere, go on, clear off!" And so, it came to pass that at about 3.30am one Monday morning a chastened, dispirited, cold and tired band of brothers meekly obeyed this instruction and cleared off through the dark and starless night.

As we trudged our weary way back to our camp, out of the blue one of our party said, "If I could get up a coach to do the return trip to London from Compton every Saturday costing only 12 shillings, instead of the official one at 18 shillings, would anyone be interested?" Naturally, everyone thought it a good idea and arrangements were made to assemble at this man's billet later in the week to finalise the deal. This was our first meeting with a man who was to become an entrepreneur long before Freddie Laker or Richard Branson came on the scene. His name was John Bloom, and he achieved fame as the man who bought out Rolls Razors and turned it into Rolls Washing Machines. He upset some of the well-established big boys like Hoover and Hotpoint by enticing the housewives with his cut-price machines, even offering a free fridge as a further inducement.

Later that week, many of us went to Bloom's billet where he was seated complete with notebook and pencil. After we had given him our name and handed over our 12 shillings, which he recorded in his book, we departed happily, looking forward to the following weekend when this exciting new enterprise was scheduled to commence. The big day came and it was a bit of a let-down when we saw a rather tired and rickety old coach turn up at the camp gate. The flight sergeant, upset at the possible loss of his trade agreement with Cards Coaches, quickly ordered it to go away and park around the corner. We didn't care and we all climbed aboard, happy at getting one over on the flight sergeant.

It seems to me the reason why people such as the Lakers, Bransons and Blooms of this world do succeed is their skill in seeing an opportunity and going for it with vision and sheer determination. On that first weekend trip to London, John Bloom, in an effort to maximise his profit margin, sat on the floor of the coach, thereby forfeiting his own seat and pocketing another 12 shillings. Bear in mind the coach floor was metal ribbed, cold, hard and most uncomfortable, especially as he sat at the front of the coach which meant he inhaled all the diesel fumes coming off the engine! I'd say he deserved every penny he made on that weekend.

On the Sunday night at London's King's Cross coach station, we all assembled for the return journey back to camp. Panic set in when there was no sign of Bloom and his coach. What some people were going to do to him is unrepeatable here, except to say they were blooming mad! Then suddenly, a loud cheer arose at the sight of our chariot, practically on two wheels, when it came roaring round the corner with our Bloom hanging out of the doorway. Relieved, we all scrambled aboard and headed westwards back to Compton, and this time we didn't have to jump out at Yatesbury camp. Thank goodness for entrepreneurs.

Northwood

By 1951, I had passed my exams at Compton Basset and, as a fully trained Teleprinter Operator (TPO), was posted to HQ Coastal Command at RAF Northwood, Middlesex. Naturally I was pleased, but at the same time sorry to leave some of the other trainees. One particular fellow I remember was a chap named Jim Kelly. The reason I remember him is that when our postings came through he was posted to RAF Jurby, which is on the Isle of Man. This raised a laugh because there is an old song which starts with the words, Has anybody here seen Kelly, K-E-Double L-Y? and ends with, Kelly from the Isle of Man. Obviously, someone in the postings office had a sense of humour when seeing Jim's surname.

For me, RAF Northwood was a blessing, as being near Greenford I could easily pop home on my days off. I remember the day those of us from Compton Basset arrived at Northwood and being confronted by a young officer who enquired, "Where are you chaps from?" Upon hearing that we were TPOs from Compton Basset, his face lit up and in a burst of unrestrained pleasure he exclaimed, "Oh, TPOs from Compton Basset. Oh, jolly good show chaps!" For days afterwards we 'chaps' were going around enquiring where all the others were from. Whenever we said we were TPOs from Compton Basset, we always received the same enthusiastic replies, each time with more enthusiasm than the last, some with additions like, "Wizard Prang" or, "Chocks away!" added for good measure.

At Northwood, our signals office was based underground on the camp and due to us working shift hours, we were billeted in a separate building in a field, a mile down the road from the camp. This enabled us to come off a night shift and get some sleep away from the hustle and bustle of life on the camp.

Our special billet had beds, a coal-fuelled boiler in the middle of the room, a kitchen with some basic cooking facilities and a bathroom. There was a regular bus service from Watford which transported us to and from the camp. Being away from the camp in a field allowed us plenty of freedom for a kick around with a football.

We had a radio in our billet and I remember us all crowding around the set one glorious night (10th July 1951 to be precise) and listening to the commentary of a boxing match, when British fighter Randolph Turpin shook the world by beating the 'invincible!' American boxer Sugar Ray Robinson, one of the greatest boxers of all time, over ten pulsating rounds to become the World Middleweight Champion. Unfortunately, Turpin's triumph didn't last long because in the return fight held in New York later that year, Robinson got his revenge and regained his title.

My time spent at Northwood was the best part of my National Service. Although I came from a fairly large family, plus spending much of my teenage days mixing with other boys in the Boys' Brigade, the experience of meeting and mixing with new people, men and women, with completely different backgrounds and accents was, for me, a wonderful learning curve. I loved to hear the different accents. It didn't matter to me whether the speaker was from any of the regions of England, Scotland, Wales or Ireland (or even Kelly from the Isle of Man!), I was fascinated. So much so that over the years I have tried, with some success at times, to imitate some of these different accents. My two biggest successes came when someone said my attempt at a Scottish accent was 'more Scottish than Angus MacTavish' (not his real name but I won't divulge his real identity). On another occasion, I had to telephone a senior officer to give him an important message. My call was answered by his Irish wife who informed me he was out. As she couldn't quite understand my normal accent, I asked her if she might understand me better if I attempted to read the message in an Irish accent. She replied, "Oh, yes please sir, that would be lovely." So, bravely (or foolishly) I put on my best Irish brogue, without once saying, "Begorrah, a'tall." Anyway, she said she understood it all and would pass it on to her husband, Seamus. I never did find out if Seamus understood it, or even got the message a'tall a'tall.

Another pleasant memory of Northwood I recall was the number of pretty WAAFs stationed there. There was one particular girl who stood out as the most attractive and all the lads fancied her but, fortunately for me (or perhaps it was just her good taste!) I was the lucky one she chose to take her out. The first date we had was when I took her to a party for one of our colleagues who was celebrating his birthday. Many at the party quite naturally over-indulged in too many glasses of the old John Barleycorn, including my date, which induced a slightly muddled mind, but, ever the true gentleman and not wishing to spoil any future dates, I escorted her safely back to camp for which she was ever grateful. Talking of drinking too much brings back another memory of Northwood and a man we had in our billet. He never went to bed without taking a gulp or three from a bottle of beer he kept beside his bed, ready for another gulp or two upon awakening the next morning.

We were very fortunate at Northwood to have had a football pitch, and I remember we had two young cricketers billeted on the camp. One was medium fast bowler Alan Moss who played for Middlesex and England, and Jim Parks who followed his father, also Jim, into the Sussex team. Jim the younger was not only a brilliant batsman, playing for England in over 40 Test matches, but later in his career he switched to being a wicket keeper where his natural athletic ability realised its full potential. His sporting prowess also extended to football, and I'll never forget the match we played with me in goal (because no one else wanted to do the job). I was doing alright until I saw Jim Parks bearing down towards me at great speed with the ball firmly at his feet and a look of determination to score a goal. That was the moment when it dawned on me why nobody else wanted to be in goal. It would be nice to say I saved his shot but, alas, the ball hit the back of the net before I could get anywhere near it. He was just a naturally gifted sportsman and a joy to watch.

The camp also had a tennis court and, on our days off duty, my best pal and I often fought out a duel. It was this same pal, Gerry, who, with me, had a bit of a shock in the summer of 1951 when we were sent on an exercise for a few days, along with the WAAF Corporal in charge of us to, of all places, the vast Royal Naval Barracks at Chatham. You can imagine the ribbing us two RAF lads received from the sailors and Wrens stationed there. Every time we came into sight we were greeted with calls of, "Here come the Brylcream boys" (Brylcream was a very popular hair cream for men which was widely advertised and promoted using male models dressed in RAF uniforms as a way of increasing their sales. As a result of this ploy, it became normal practice amongst the general public to call all RAF personnel 'the Brylcream boys'). After a while we got used to the comment and even enjoyed it, particularly if it came from a Wren.

We were treated very well at Chatham and were a little sorry when the four-day exercise finished and it was time for us to return to camp. The WAAF Corporal in charge of us told us to make our own way back. As it happened, my pal lived near Wimbledon and the annual Wimbledon Tennis Championship was in full swing, so we decided this was an opportunity we couldn't miss. So, with our hair gleaming with Brylcream, we headed for the Mecca of Tennis.

I remember walking into these hallowed grounds for the first time and marvelling at the pristine condition of the grass courts. There was a feeling of excitement and anticipation in the air of what was in store for the spectators. We watched an American player called Art Larsen arriving for a practise knock-up on one of the many outside courts. What surprised us was that as he approached the baseline, he was not only smoking but he threw down his lit cigarette just behind the baseline and proceeded to practise as if this was normal. This sort of cavalier attitude went completely against the well-established etiquette expected at Wimbledon, but no one seemed to reprimand him. Apparently, he was an inveterate smoker but this didn't impair his tennis ability. He made it through to the quarter finals before being knocked out. The respective winners that year were two Americans; Dick Savitt, winning the men's title, and Doris Hart the ladies'. We were also lucky in seeing another great American player Budge Patty beat Swedish player Sven Davidson in an exciting match.

Seeing Wimbledon for the first time was something I've never forgotten and in all my subsequent years watching this ultra-British spectacle on television brings back those fond memories from 1951. Unfortunately, Gerry and I were enjoying our visit so much that we slightly overstayed, resulting in it taking longer than we thought to get back to camp. Our late arrival was duly recorded and the next day our warrant officer summoned us to his office, enquiring about the reason for our lateness. We meekly apologised and somehow talked ourselves out of it, but it was a close call.

Being Demobbed

On 28th March 1952, the RAF decided the country could manage without me and I was duly released from my two years' National Service and returned to Civvy Street. My parents were delighted and somewhat proud of the fact that all of their five children had served the country in the armed forces. My father had of course served in the army throughout the First World War and had somehow survived the horrors of the Western front. My eldest brother, Bert, was next, serving with the Eighth Army at El Alamein in the Middle East in the Second World War. My sister Lily joined the ATS and helped defend London by assisting on the Ack Ack guns. Bernard was also in the army, serving as a member of the Parachute Regiment and sent to Palestine during the troubles there in 1947. Next was David, who, despite hating most of his time in the army, did at least do his National Service duty and, lastly, it was my turn to leave mother and home to complete the circle. Lily, David and I were lucky in so much as we didn't get sent overseas to a war zone, although I came close and was extremely lucky not to have been sent to Korea in 1951.

I remember my dad saying no one could say our family hadn't done their bit for our country.

It was a bittersweet moment when I was demobbed and had to leave all my friends at Northwood. You meet so many different characters and personalities, men and women from all sorts of backgrounds, with different standards and opinions, some not compatible with yours but others completely in harmony with your views. Of course, this then makes it all the harder to say goodbye, but there are many who you never really forget.

After being demobbed from the RAF and spending a brief time at home, I returned to my old job – shoe repairing at the Express Shoe Repairs shop in Greenford. I found it difficult to settle back into this life again. My experience was nothing compared to the thousands, even millions of those who had been away fighting overseas, many coming home traumatised with injuries – both physical and mental – from their experiences, whether on battlefields or as prisoners of war. The hardships and agonies they and their families endured trying to readjust to their earlier lifestyle had become something foreign, and for many was never quite the same again. It certainly made me realise how lucky I was.

After a few weeks at the shop I spoke to my boss and told him how I felt. He said he fully understood and wouldn't try to dissuade me if I wanted to leave. He wished me luck for the future and I left the world of cobbling behind, although I must say, my ability to repair shoes was useful in my early days of marriage when money was a bit tight.

Chapter 10

Working Life

The American Embassy

Before the RAF introduced me to the world of teleprinters I hardly knew anything about these machines. I certainly wasn't aware of how much they were used in the world of communications, not just in the armed services, but also in civilian life. Many men and women learnt the necessary skills through the training they received through the armed services, but also in civilian life with companies such as the Post Office, Western Union, Commercial Cable Company and PQ. This quick way of communicating was also used by newspapers, banks and shipping companies. This hit home with me and many of my colleagues when one of our colleagues from Northwood was demobbed and got a job at the American Embassy in London, putting his teleprinting skills to work and getting paid £7 per week, which in the 1950s was a good wage. There was one subtle difference, though – the American system didn't use teleprinters as we knew them. Their machines were called Teletype machines, which were different in design and layout but basically did the same thing, so didn't pose too many problems adapting to them.

Upon learning this information, I decided that when I was demobbed, I would also apply for a job at the American Embassy in London. I subsequently did this and was successful in being invited to the Embassy for an interview.

Dressed in my best suit and with my hair beautifully Brylcreamed, I marched through the portals of this smart modern building in Grosvenor Square and was ushered into a room where I faced my interviewer. He was a very pleasant and polite man who had my job application form on his desk. He asked me various questions about my upbringing and interests but when I told him that in my youth I had been a member of the Boys' Brigade, he looked a bit startled. This meeting was taking place in June 1952, a time when the threat of Communist spies infiltrating America was causing widespread panic and unrest and a prominent senator by the name of Joseph McCarthy was conducting massive witch hunts throughout the country. So, the fact that I had been in the Boys' Brigade solicited this worrying question from my interviewer, "What is this Boys' Brigade, some kind of group activity to overthrow the government?" He had never heard of the organisation, but when I explained it was no different to the Boy Scout movement he was placated.

My application was accepted and I started working at the American Embassy in June 1952. On reflection, I thought it's a good job I never mentioned the Mohawks,

Zulus, Eskimos and the Hottentots at my interview! I would probably have been thrown out.

Once I had settled in at the Embassy, I quickly adapted to the Teletype machines and I enjoyed the new working environment. We had a nice mixture of British operators backed up by some Americans handling all the clerical desk work. I must say the Americans were very easy to work with and generous, dishing out goodies, especially at Christmas when they surprised us all by coming into our working room loaded with cigarettes, chocolates, candies and a bottle or two of bourbon, gin, rum or beer, anything to ensure everyone had a very 'merry' Christmas. But, surprisingly, this job wasn't to last long for me. This quick change came about because one of my new colleagues at the Embassy had previously worked for Shell in London and the stories he told me of how good the company were to work for made me think. Shell offered free meals, sport facilities and best of all, a very solid pension scheme. Why my colleague left, I couldn't tell you! So, although I enjoyed my time at the Embassy, I decided that perhaps in the long run I would be better off with Shell. At the end of December 1952, I said goodbye to all my buddies at the Embassy and joined the Shell Petroleum Company (as it was called in those days), at their London Head Office in St Helen's Court, Bishopsgate.

Shell

My decision to leave the American Embassy proved to be a good move because, in January 1953, the ex-General and Allied Supreme Commander during the

Second World War, Dwight David Eisenhower, was inaugurated as the new President of the United States. One of the first decisions his new administration made was to cut back on staff levels at many of the US Embassies around the world. This drastic move included the Embassy in London, where the last three people to join the communications department were made redundant. As I had been one of those last three, it was very fortuitous that I jumped ship before I was pushed.

Moving from working in Grosvenor Square, a modern and upmarket area of London, to working in the City of London, an older and more sedate area but one steeped in banking history and world famous as the financial capital of the world, was quite a change. This was an area of London new to me and I enjoyed wandering around, exploring such places as St Paul's Cathedral, Monument, Ludgate Circus and Fleet Street. Shell had moved into St Helen's Court in 1914 and decided to make it their London headquarters. It was quite an imposing building and I remember entering the marbled grand entrance of the building for the first time to be greeted by a very upright uniformed commissionaire. I also noted one of the walls proudly displayed a long roll of honour commemorating the names of all the Shell personnel who had lost their lives during the First World War. This was the beginning of my 36-year-long career with the company.

My daily journey to St Helen's Court entailed travelling on the underground Central line from Greenford to Bank station, and walking up Threadneedle Street into Bishopgate to St Helen's Court and the Shell offices.

I was made very welcome by the existing staff members, both male and female. Many of them, like me, had undergone TPO training in the services or at the Post Office. Our office was a bit old fashioned in style and furniture and discipline was strict, as was the dress code. Men wore suits and ties along with polished shoes, and the ladies, who had endured the wartime lack of choice in clothes due to the rationing, although welcoming the new styles which were coming onto the scene, still had to dress in what was called, 'a quiet, dignified and tasteful manner, suitable for the office environment they were working in'.

Another of the Shell benefits available to all the staff was just a walk away from St Helen's Court. This was a large emporium called Houndsditch Warehouse. It was a veritable Aladdin's cave selling a vast array of household items, all at greatly reduced prices.

By the time I started at Shell, I was an uncle three times over. My brother Bernard and his wife Joan had a daughter, Valerie, followed by my sister Lily and her husband Jack, who had their first child, a boy given the Welsh name Gareth (Gary), due to Jack being a proud Welshman. The third arrival came when my eldest brother, Bert, and his wife Ethel also had a daughter, named Elaine.

My birthplace, Bettws
Cedewen, 1931

Me (bottom left) with my
parents and siblings, 1935

VE Day street party for the children. David
(middle row, 4th from left) and me (same row
3rd from right in a striped shirt), Greenford, 1945

Me (back row, far right) in the Boys' Brigade Team London
West Middlesex Battalion Football Championship 1948-49

Boys' Brigade badge

Me, aged 20

Me at the Royal Air
Force Station Northwood,
Middlesex, 1951

Me with RAF comrade Gerry Halls having a National
'Service' tennis break at RAF Northwood, 1951

Me playing my guitar with friends from Shell.
Hayes, Kent, 1957

Me with two Shell colleagues, Frank Hill
and Ron Jeffery, 1957

Me with my wife-to-be Kathy
at Butlin's Clacton, 1958

Kathy and I on our wedding
day, Greenford, 27th
December 1958

Our wedding, Greenford Methodist Church,
27th December 1958

1937 LANCHESTER 14
PAID £27-50 SOLD £15-00
USED 1962-63

Lanchester 14 HP 1937. Pre-selector
gearbox with fluid flywheel

The Green Flash at Heron Close, Church Crookham

My sons Chris and Martin in Austria, 1970

Me with my brothers and father, 1973

Kathy ready for another shift as a ward sister, 1973

My first caravan in the New Forest, with my
two sons and niece present, 1974

Me and my guitar with fellow caravanner Bill
with his piano accordion at a caravan rally,
Hampshire, 1970s

The ship loved by many British cruisers,
Canberra, in dock, late 1970s

Me with my brothers Bernard, Dave,
Bert, and my sister, Lily, 1978

The overall front shot of Shell
centre, 1970s

Me at Shell, 1978

Me and my pipe, Shell
Centre, 1978

Me with my Rollieflex at Shell
Centre, 1970s

On a caravan rally
Bagshot Lea, Surrey, 1979

Me, 1980

Christmas caravanning at Marwell,
near Winchester, Hampshire, early 1980s

Full steam ahead at sea on another cruise

My caravan outfit; Ford Granada, Avondale caravan
with awning deployed, 1982

Invitation we received for a cruise to the
West Indies to celebrate my birthday

Me singing at a caravan rally in Hindhead, Surrey, 1983

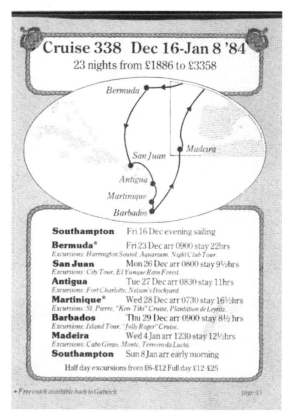

Cruise 338 Dec 16-Jan 8 '84
23 nights from £1886 to £3358

Southampton   Fri 16 Dec evening sailing
Bermuda*   Fri 23 Dec arr 0900 stay 22hrs
Excursions: Harrington Sound, Aquarium, Night Club Tour.
San Juan   Mon 26 Dec arr 0800 stay 9½hrs
Excursions: City Tour, El Yunque Rain Forest.
Antigua   Tue 27 Dec arr 0830 stay 11hrs
Excursions: Fort Charlotte, Nelson's Dockyard.
Martinique*   Wed 28 Dec arr 0730 stay 16½hrs
Excursions: St. Pierre, "Kon-Tiki" Cruise, Plantation de Leyritz.
Barbados   Thu 29 Dec arr 0900 stay 8½ hrs
Excursions: Island Tour, "Jolly Roger" Cruise.
Madeira   Wed 4 Jan arr 1230 stay 12½hrs
Excursions: Cabo Girao, Monte, Terreiro da Lucta.
Southampton   Sun 8 Jan arr early morning

Half day excursions from £6-£12 Full day £12-£25

• Free coach available back to Gatwick   page 15

Itinerary of a great cruise we enjoyed

Maiden voyage of the Royal Princess, 1984

Caravan BBQ rally alongside the Thames at
Windsor, mid 1980s

Keeping fit at sea

Royal Marines band preforming to another liner
leaving Southampton docks

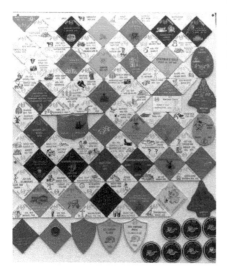

Some of the many plaques given out for attending Caravan Club rallies

Pub meal with friends Terry and Joy, at the local pub the Haymaker, Combe St Nicolas, Somerset, late 1980s

Alcatraz Island, taken on our trip, 1990

Grand Canyon, 1990

Our visit to the Grand Canyon with our friend Joy, 1990

One of our US holidays, Yukon, 1990s

Two of my brothers, Bert (middle) playing the
tenor saxophone and Bernard (left) on the trumpet,
with friend Chris Jacques on clarinet (who also
played in Bernard's New City Jazzman)

John Stringfellows was the inventor of flight in 1848.
Chard, Somerset

Me with good friend Joy and another member of the
Chard Light Operatic Society in a production of Oklahoma!

The farm food shop at Cricket St Thomas
Wildlife Park, Somerset

Martin's business, Chapplins, April 1996

Lyme Regis, Dorset, a place frequently
visited by Kathy and me

I spotted my namesake on a Welsh holiday

Approaching my birthplace, Powys, Wales

Commandos Second World War Memorial in the Scottish Highlands near Spean Bridge, which is about eight miles north east of Fort William

Kathy's mother, Cecelia Gunner, Burgh le Marsh,
near Skegness, 2002

Martin, me and Michael, Liphook Golf Course, 2005

Chris and Martin standing outside The British
Touch, Shakespeare, Ontario, Canada

Chris at home in Canada

The P&O cruise ship Aurora,
one of our favourite ships, 2006

With my brothers Bernard and David, celebrating
Bernard's 80th birthday, Crawley, West Sussex, 2007

Chris outside The British Touch, Shakespeare, Ontario

Chris at his shop The British Touch

Kathy with grandaughter Nicole at
The British Touch, Canada

Grandaughter Nicole, 2007

Me with my two sons at Tavistock
Golf Club, Ontario, Canada, 2007

A Lake Huron sunset, Ontario, Canada.
Photo taken by me

Another Lake Huron sunset, Ontario,
Canada. Photo by me, 2007

Kathy and me at a family get together at Bayfield,
Ontario, Canada, 2008

Golden wedding anniversary celebration dinner, 2008

Me and Bernard getting a taste for our dad's
printing days at Gregynog Hall

Gregynog Hall, Tregynon, Powys

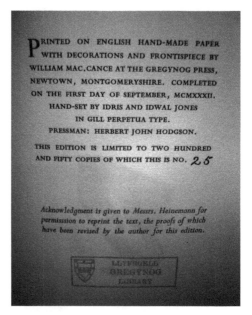

PRINTED ON ENGLISH HAND-MADE PAPER
WITH DECORATIONS AND FRONTISPIECE BY
WILLIAM MAC.CANCE AT THE GREGYNOG PRESS,
NEWTOWN, MONTGOMERYSHIRE. COMPLETED
ON THE FIRST DAY OF SEPTEMBER, MCMXXXII.
HAND-SET BY IDRIS AND IDWAL JONES
IN GILL PERPETUA TYPE.
PRESSMAN: HERBERT JOHN HODGSON.

THIS EDITION IS LIMITED TO TWO HUNDRED
AND FIFTY COPIES OF WHICH THIS IS NO. 25

*Acknowledgment is given to Messrs. Heinemann for
permission to reprint the text, the proofs of which
have been revised by the author for this edition.*

Credit reference to one of the fine art books printed
by my father, Herbert Hodgson

Museum display showing the general public what to
watch out for at the advent of the Second World War
in southern England

Visit to British car day, Oakville, Ontario, Canada, 2008

Taken by me from our kitchen window, Chard, Somerset

Another taken by me from our kitchen window,
Chard, Somerset

Two of the
grandchildren, Laura
and Michael, at their
home in Hampshire,
2009

Clive Price (one of my nephews) playing one of my
father's mandolin banjos at Gregynog Hall, 2010

The Hodgson family meeting up with descendants
of Richard Cook, the owner of the lost Bible,
Etaples, France, 8th October 2010

Me receiving the lost Bible from my older brother Bernard

Martin reading the lost Bible with his son and daughter

Me reflecting on the story of the lost Bible found by
my father during the First World War, 1st January 2011

Me handing over the lost Bible to my brother David,
ready to take it to New Zealand

David Hodgson passing Richard Cook's (Kiwi soldier)
lost Bible to Colonel Seymour in New Zealand
on the last stage of its journey home, 2011

Display of the lost Bible in the National Army Museum,
Waiouru, New Zealand with commerative plaques
of Herbert Hodgson and Richard Cook

Kathy and I, 2011

My 80th birthday
present from
my sons

Dining together on a WI trip to Holland

From left, Martin, Chris, Lois, me, Kathy, Michael,
Laura and Nicole at Salisbury Cathedral, Wiltshire, 2012

Dubrovnik, Croatia, 2015

Kathy with her brothers, Colin and Peter

Kathy's lifelong friend, Heather, and husband,
Paul, on a walk in autumn leaves, Sidcup, Kent

Me driving off at The Windwhistle Golf Club,
Chard, Somerset, 2017

Forde Abbey, Dorset. Another photo by me

Forde Abbey, Dorset. Photo by me

Gravestone of T.E Lawrence (Lawrence of Arabia)
Moreton Churchyard, near Wareham, Dorset, 2018

Me with the captain of the Oceana, receiving the card from the Queen celebrating Kathy and my Diamond wedding anniversay (with the cake in the background)

Diamond wedding anniversary cake baked onboard the P&O Oceana cruise ship, with the Queen's congratulations card, 2018

Photo by me at the popular National Trust
property Stourhead, Wiltshire

Photo by me of Lulworth Cove, Dorset

Chapter 11

Mid-1950s Britain

Events of the Mid-1950s

The year 1953 began rather miserably when, on 31st January, the east coast of England was battered by hurricane force winds and high tides bringing devastation from Lincolnshire down as far as Kent. Hundreds were killed and thousands made homeless. One report said around 100 people in Canvey Island, Essex, were drowned, 500 missing and thousands were evacuated. In Clacton, also in Essex, holiday chalets were swamped under 12 foot of water, in Norfolk 12 American servicemen were reportedly among 60 drowned, and in neighbouring Suffolk boats were rowed into a church to rescue 40 trapped children.

Serial killer John Christie was arrested and hanged at the Old Bailey, having been charged with the murders of at least eight women, including his wife. He carried out these killings at his home – 10 Rillington Place, in the Notting Hill area of London. Christie buried all his victims in the garden. This horrific and gruesome story made history and was made into a film (1971) where the part of Christie was portrayed by Richard Attenbough, and was later made into a TV series in 2016.

Fortunately, the year wasn't all gloom and tragedy. On the sporting field, one of Britain's all-time greatest footballers, Stanley Matthews (later to become the first footballer to be knighted), won his first winner's medal in the Cup Final. In a thrilling match against Bolton Wanderers at Wembley Stadium, with Bolton leading 3-1 with only 20 minutes to go, Matthews turned on a display of such brilliance that Blackpool scored three more goals and finished as 4-3 winners. This virtuoso performance by Matthews was so outstanding that the match became for ever known as 'The Matthews Final'.

The champion jockey Gordon Richards had never won the Derby race before, but glory came when he won his first Derby riding a horse called Pinza. Just when we all thought you can't beat that, along came the English cricket team who not only dramatically beat the Aussies in the final match at the Oval when golden boy Denis Compton hit the winning run, it also meant England had regained the Ashes after 19 years. Captain of England was Yorkshire's wonderful batsman Len Hutton, who made history by being the first professional cricket player to captain England.

There was great joy amongst the children of Britain in 1953 when, for the second time since the war, all confectionary was taken off of rationing, and this time it stayed off.

The biggest event of the year occurred on 2nd June, when the Coronation of Queen Elizabeth II took place.

The ceremony in Westminster Abbey and the street processions before and afterwards were examples of Britain at its best. Despite the rainy weather, the sheer pomp, pageantry and splendour of this tradition was watched with pride and fascination by thousands lining the route to the Abbey, and millions more around the world due to the wonders of television. My parents decided, just as we had done during the war years with our Anderson shelter, to invite our neighbours in to watch this happy event on our television set, even though in those days the picture was in black and white.

One of the best-remembered sights of that day was Queen Salote of Tonga, who captivated everyone with her big smile, despite her open carriage filling up with the rainwater! The vast crowds outside Buckingham Palace cheered and waved Union Jacks as the newly crowned Queen and Prince Philip appeared six times on the balcony in acknowledgement and gratitude to the crowds, who stayed outside waving and cheering even after the couple made their final appearance at midnight. The well-known, and sometimes derided, British reserve was cast to the wind as bowler hats on umbrellas were waved, balloons were released and, along the Thames Embankment, fireworks zoomed off in the night sky, which was a fitting climax to an unforgettable day in our rich and proud history.

Just when we thought nothing could surpass that historic day, news came through that Mount Everest had finally been conquered. New Zealander Edmund Hillary and Sherpa Tensing from Nepal, both members of Colonel John Hunt's expedition team, had made it to the summit on 29th May 1953. Although the news had been held back due to the Coronation.

The Wimbledon tournament in 1953 saw a new star burst onto the scene when an young American named Maureen Connelly who, due to her diminutive height, was lovingly dubbed Little Mo, won the ladies' title, beating fellow American Doris Hart in the final. The men's title was won by another American, Vic Seixas, who beat Denmark's Kurt Nielsen.

The American dominance in sport continued into the world of golf when one of the best-ever golfers, Ben Hogan, made his one and only appearance in the Open Championship, and conquered Scotland's windswept Carnoustie course to win the most coveted trophy in golf.

Without doubt the biggest shock came later in the year when the Hungarian football team came to Wembley and gave us a lesson in free-flowing football, which we in Britain had never witnessed before. They beat us 6-3 and became the first team to defeat England on their own ground. At the end of the game, the stunned crowd slowly filed out of the stadium in a state of bewilderment. I know this because I, along with my brother Bernard, was one of those poor unfortunate souls. Incidentally, England's right back that momentous day was Alf Ramsay, the man who eventually became manager of the England team and guided them to winning the World Cup in 1966.

Probably one of the most beneficial discoveries for mankind happened in 1953, when British physicist

Francis Crick and American James Watson uncovered the secrets of DNA. Their breakthrough, aided by New Zealander Maurice Wilkins, was justly rewarded in 1962 when the three men won the Nobel Prize for Medicine.

On the sporting front, 1954 is best remembered as the year when Britain's Roger Bannister became the first man to run a mile in under four minutes. At an Oxford race meeting, and helped by colleagues Chris Chataway and Chris Basher, he finished the race in 3 minutes 59.4 seconds.

The FA Cup that year was won by West Bromwich Albion, who beat Preston North End 3-2. Czech tennis player Jaroslav Drobny won the Wimbledon men's title and American Little Mo Connelly won the ladies' title for the second year running. Australian golfer Peter Thomson easily won the Open and champion jockey Gordon Richards became Sir Gordon when he was knighted by the Queen, the first jockey to receive such an honour. Talking of jockeys, an 18-year-old lad by the name of Lester Piggott became the youngest jockey ever to win the Derby when he rode Never Say Die first past the post. Lester Piggott eventually went on to win another eight Derby races and became one of the best jockeys of all time.

In April 1955, Winston Churchill, the man who inspired millions around the world throughout the dark and frightening days of the Second World War, at 80 years of age resigned as Britain's Prime Minister. His deputy, Anthony Eden, took over the reins.

In the same year, the world lost Sir Alexander Fleming, who died in July 1955. He discovered Penicillin in 1928 and for which he – along with Australian pathologist Howard Florey and German biochemist Ernst Chain – received the Nobel Prize for Physiology or Medicine in 1945. In complete contrast to these three men whose work did so much to save lives, in the same month of Fleming's death Ruth Ellis also made history when she was convicted for murdering her lover and became the last woman to be hung in Britain.

One of the worst things that resulted from the war was the number of unexploded bombs which lay undiscovered beneath fields, buildings and beaches throughout the country for many years afterwards. Many disasters occurred when one of these bombs was disturbed and exploded. One such incident happened when five schoolboys found an unexploded bomb on a beach in Swanage, Dorset. They tried to prise off the top of the bomb when it exploded, killing all of them. Even as I write this in 2021, these hidden death-traps are still being discovered, usually when excavations for new buildings are being carried out.

In 1955, Cardiff was chosen as the capital city of Wales. Naturally, the valleys and beyond were filled with the sound of the many choirs celebrating the news. So, it really was, 'Yakki Da and Cymru au Byth' which roughly translated means, 'Goodbye and Wales for ever.'

The year 1956 produced some unforgettable sporting events. In the world of cricket, Yorkshire's brilliant batsman Len Hutton was awarded a Knighthood and fellow Yorkshireman, spin bowler Jim Laker, made history when in a Test match against the Australians at Old Trafford he took a total of 19 wickets. He took 9 for 90 in their first innings and 10 for 53 in the second, becoming the first man to take all 10 wickets in a Test match. I remember the sheer excitement, watching this outstanding performance along with some friends on the old black and white television screen as the wickets tumbled.

Sadly, not all sporting events end in triumph and this was very evident when in the same year at the Grand National, the Queen Mother's horse, Devon Loch, who had jumped all the fences without any sign of trouble, suddenly collapsed as it neared the winning post, allowing another horse, E.S.B, to emerge as the winner. The reason for the fall was never really discovered.

Popular cars in Britain at this time included the Ford Anglia, Prefect, Consul and the Zephyr/Zodiac, followed closely by the Hillman Minx, Standard 10, Morris Oxford and the much-loved Morris Minor, which started production in 1948 and sold well over 1.3 million cars before production ceased in 1972. Another car which raised a few eyebrows was the arrival of the three wheel 'bubble' cars. There was the Isetta and the Messerschmitt from BMW which, despite only having a 250cc engine, still managed speeds of between 60-70 mph, and, also, the Heinkel. None of these cars were around for any length of time so I suppose you could say it didn't take long before the 'bubble' burst. Britain during the 1950s was a golden time for motorcycles with sidecars. It was quite a common sight to see a couple or a family taking to the roads for a trip to the coast or into the countryside for a day out on one of these. A family would have the dad driving, suitably equipped with a pair of goggles and leather gloves, with the mother sitting behind him, her arms wrapped around his waist, whilst the face of an excited child peered out from the window of the sidecar.

In November 1956, the Chancellor of the Exchequer at that time, Harold Macmillan, introduced Premium Bonds which were scheduled to go on sale on 1st June 1957. This was a government backed investment scheme where for £1 you could buy a Premium Bond which bore a unique number and was entered into a monthly draw with a top prize of £1,000 and prizes of a smaller value down to £10 if your numbered bond was drawn. The maximum number of bonds anyone could have was 250. The scheme took off, far exceeding the government's expectations (on the first day of issue there were five million pounds worth of bonds sold) and, as I write this over 60 years later, it is still going strong. The big differences now are that the maximum holding anyone can have has increased to £50,000. The lowest prize is now £25 and the jackpot is £1million. Every month there are two draws which give the chance for two lucky people to win the jackpot prize.

The beauty of Premium Bonds is that although they don't accrue any interest on your investment, they are redeemable at face value at any time, so you always get your original stake money back, albeit it won't be worth as much in time due to inflation. I have won a few smaller prizes over the years but am still awaiting the 'big' one!

Music in the 1950s

During these early days of the 1950s in Britain, there was a revival of traditional jazz music which had started in the late 1940s. By this time, I was a dedicated devotee to this brand of music. This was due to my brother Bernard who fell in love with trad jazz from an early age, so much so that he became a trumpet player himself and formed his own trad band. From him I learnt about jazz artists such as Bunk Johnson, Jelly Roll Morton, King Oliver, George Lewis, and the one and only Louis Armstrong. One of the highlights of my later life was seeing Louis, or Satchmo as he was lovingly called, when he gave a concert with his All Stars Band at London's Earls Court in 1955. I was in heaven seeing and hearing this supreme artist who injected so much feeling into his music. I only have to hear a few notes from his trumpet to know its Louis. His artistry and influence on the world of music was acknowledged and appreciated by musicians from all genres.

To me, it doesn't matter one iota what style or choice of music a musician performs. Like the written or spoken word, if the overall sound stirs one of the many emotions lying dormant within all of us, be it happiness, sadness, excitement, longing, melancholy, inspiring, hope or encouragement, then the writer, composer or performer, in my opinion, has done their job.

British cornet player Ken Colyer was once a merchant seaman and was fortunate enough on one trip to visit New Orleans. When he subsequently formed his own band, the Ken Colyer Jazzmen, around 1953/1954, he just had to pay homage to the home of trad jazz by recording an LP (long playing) record called *New Orleans to London*. The opening track on this record was appropriately called *Going Home* and included the lyrics, If home is where the heart is then my home's in New Orleans. This record is considered by many as the best ever British trad jazz record. Although I can't remember what price it was to buy when it came out, probably around the £2 mark, I bought a copy and played and treasured it for many years. Eventually I transferred it onto an audio cassette tape which I still have. With the passing of time and the phasing out of record players, I decided to sell my original record. I advertised it on eBay and got £25 for it.

Also in 1955, disc jockey Jack Jackson started giving a lot of airtime to a record called *The Rock Island Line* by Lonnie Donegan. At the time of Lonnie Donegan's hit record he was a member of the Chris Barber Jazz Band (which it had become when Ken Colyer left). Pat Halcox was brought in as trumpet/cornet player and formed a partnership with the Chris Barber Band which lasted for 54 years, only ending with Pat's death in February 2013. I was very lucky that through my brother Bernard's involvement with jazz, I met Pat Halcox on a few occasions. Not only was he a wonderful trumpet player with great feeling and imagination, he was also one of the nicest people you could ever meet.

Lonnie Donegan's recording of *The Rock Island Line* introduced a new sound to Britain – skiffle – and it swept the country. Skiffle is a blend of folk and country music, with influences from traditional jazz and blues.

To play skiffle was relatively easy. Obviously, you had to have some ability to sing, hopefully in tune to a certain degree, although it must be said that in many cases that basic requirement was not always present! The instruments were a guitar or two, a double bass and a washboard. Thousands of young lads dashed out to purchase a guitar and started to learn three basic chords: C, F and B7 (known as the three-chord trick). Once this was mastered, you could use these chords to accompany many simple folk and country songs. The double bass was another story, as the cost of buying one of these monsters was out of the question, so a cheap alternative was to buy or 'acquire' a wooden tea chest, a broom handle and a length of string. Just a washboard was needed to complete the ensemble. Having obtained one, you fixed thimbles to your fingers and ran them up and down the grooved metal edges. These three instruments produced a great rhythm section and youths all over the country were forming their own skiffle groups. Popular songs were attacked with great gusto and enthusiasm, if little musicianship!

To add to the new phenomenon of skiffle hitting Britain, another craze was to follow with the advent of Teddy Boys. Originating from the 1940s, this was the name given to teenage boys who wore a style of clothes originally worn during the Edwardian period. This sartorial style consisted of long drape jackets with a velvet collar, drainpipe trousers and varying colours of shirt topped off with a bootlace tie. Often, they would wear brightly coloured socks with suede (usually blue) shoes which had very thick crepe soles. This type of footwear quickly became known as 'brothel creepers' (having never had any desire to visit such establishments I cannot vouch for the authenticity of that description!). To complete their ensemble, these lads had haircuts with huge quiffs and sideburns and the obligatory chewing gum and cigarette completed the image. The phrase 'Teddy Boys' passed into everyday language and is still used today, often unjustly, by older people describing present-day, unusually attired teenagers.

I was lucky enough to meet Lonnie once. He had just returned from a tour of America and was playing at Prince of Wales Theatre in London. The show was sold out and my friend Dickie Bishop and I were allowed to wait in Lonnie's dressing room until the show had finished. Lonnie came off stage and, after a brief rest, regaled us with hilarious tales from his recent tour.

Whilst I enjoyed many of Lonnie's skiffle songs, there is one number which, for me, is his best. Unlike the others, this one comes from a Broadway show and subsequent film, *Bells are Ringing*. The song is called *The Party's Over*, and the lyrics went, It's time to call it a day. Lonnie sang this lovely song very slowly and with great feeling and emotion. It was a world away from many of his usual skiffle numbers. Unfortunately, the party was finally over on 3rd November 2012, when Lonnie, who was halfway through a UK tour, collapsed and died from a heart attack, aged 71.

Other singers making the girls swoon were Marty Wilde, Terry Dene, Billy Fury and Adam Faith, who went on to become a very good actor. Finally, there was Harry Webb, the Peter Pan of pop music who changed his name to Cliff Richard and who, much later in life, became Sir Cliff and is still singing as I write this. This pop culture, coupled with the mixture of skiffle and trad jazz, gave the teenagers (not to mention some of us more mature people) plenty of variety to choose from.

It was also around this time that many American singers started coming over to appear at the London Palladium. I remember the American actor, singer and comedian Danny Kaye came over to perform at the Palladium. He took London by storm, completely captivating the audience just by sitting on a chair near the orchestra pit and sipping from a cup of tea and chatting. Every now and again he jumped up to the microphone and sang a song or two before sitting down for some more chatting. It was so relaxed and informal, just as if he was in your lounge at home. Even Princess Margaret made two visits to see him perform.

In 1951 whilst on leave from the Royal Air Force, I visited the Palladium again where I saw another icon of the entertainment world, the one and only Judy Garland who took everyone 'somewhere over the rainbow'. This hit song from her 1939 film *The Wizard of Oz* became her signature tune. It also has a special significance for me which comes later in my story.

My love for the theatre, especially musical theatre, continued and I visited the London Palladium many times during the middle of the 1950s to see singers and comedians such as Eddie Fisher, Frankie Laine, Billy Daniels, Kay Starr, Dean Martin and Jerry Lewis and the clap happy singer, Guy Mitchell. Other great artists

I saw included the wonderfully droll Jack Benny, who could illicit a smile from his audience just by looking at them without a saying a word. Britain's Max Bygraves, George Formby and Frankie Howerd were also popular entertainers at that time. Every Sunday evening the Ted Heath Band (not to be confused with Edward Heath who was Britain's Prime Minister between 1970-1974) with his singers Dickie Valentine, Lita Roza and Dennis Lotis would give a big band concert.

I consider myself very lucky that I can enjoy a wide variety of music, ranging from trad jazz to classical, and through my father's and eldest brother's musical background, I grew up hearing and appreciating the wonderful melodies written by popular composers. I've also been lucky to hear and enjoy singers from all sides of the musical divide, whether it's Pavarotti or Maria Callas from the world of opera, Hank Williams Snr and John Denver from the country scene, or Ella Fitzgerald (especially when joining with Louis Armstrong), Nat King Cole, Frank Sinatra, Bing Crosby, Tony Bennett, Perry Como, Dean Martin and Britain's own Matt Monro from the world of popular music. Their songs brought pleasure to millions around the world. Thank goodness they left us many recordings.

When skiffle arrived, I was also caught up in it and joined the craze by buying my first guitar. This came about through another friend of Bernard's, Dickie Bishop, who played banjo occasionally with the Barber band, and guitar with Lonnie Donegan. Dickie had decided to change his guitar for another model and asked me if I'd like to buy his old model. As it was a Gibson, I jumped at the chance.

I was also lucky that my brother Bert, who played saxophone and clarinet and had formed his own dance band, put me in touch with a brilliant guitar player by the name of Bert Kirby. I had lessons for the princely sum of 10 shillings per lesson. The long hours of practising resulted in me mastering about six chords and suffering very red indented fingers, but the suffering was worthwhile because it meant that not only was I able to accompany myself when singing some of the skiffle and country songs, I was also able to play my guitar with my father on his mandolin banjo. We made up the rhythm section, whilst Bert on sax and Bernard on trumpet provided the melodies for the rest of the family to sing along to at the annual Hodgson Christmas festivities. What wonderful happy memories I have of those joyful occasions.

At that same time I was learning to play the guitar, I was also having driving lessons. I would have a guitar lesson in the evening and a driving lesson during the day. There was one memorable moment when I was having a driving lesson the morning after a guitar lesson. I was driving along quite comfortably when the instructor gave me an instruction that I didn't quite hear, so he repeated it, and I responded, "Sorry, I forgot what key I was in," instead of what gear I was in. The incredulous look on the instructor's face was a sight to behold. I imagined him telling his fellow instructors back at the driving centre about the idiot he taught today who forgot what key he was in. It wouldn't surprise me to learn that somewhere my name is included in a driving instructor's manual entitled *Idiots I've Taught*.

My love for trad jazz continued and when Bernard and his band were engaged to perform every Sunday afternoon at the Hamborough Tavern in Hayes, Middlesex, I would go along and help out by taking the money at the door whilst enjoying the music for free.

The year 1956 was notable as the year when Britain faced another explosion on the music scene, when a young man from Mississippi burst upon us and changed the face of pop music. Yes, I'm talking about Elvis Presley, who entered the hit parade with a song called *Heartbreak Hotel* and, later that year, *Blue Suede Shoes*, *Hound Dog*, *Don't be Cruel* and *Love Me Tender*.

Teenagers in Britain were soon rushing out to buy his records. The gyrating and somewhat sensual body movements this man performed whilst singing his songs on stage caused raised eyebrows to say the least amongst the older generations around the world, but as far as the young people were concerned, he was fantastic and idolised.

There were many other Elvis worshippers who couldn't sing a note, at least not in tune, or play the guitar, but that was of no consequence. All they had to do was to follow Elvis's dress code, which included blue suede shoes, and remember to carry a comb which they frequently used to comb their hair into a special style known as having a 'DA'. This was an abbreviation of a personal part of a duck's anatomy! Armed with this transformation, the 'poor man's Elvis' would gyrate around like a whirling dervish, causing the girls to swoon and scream their heads off.

Another performer who caused riots in Britain at this time was Bill Haley & His Comets, who burst onto the scene with a record called *Rock Around the Clock* which topped the hit parade for many years afterwards. Bill Haley was older than Elvis and with a 'kiss curl' haircut; he differed to Elvis's thick black hair. There were many occasions when the police were called out to cinemas to stop the youngsters rocking and rolling in the aisles, and then in the streets after being evicted from the cinemas.

The hit parade records of this period could be heard from record players, Dansette being one popular make, in many homes throughout the country. In complete contrast to rock and roll records, we had crooner Pat Boone telling us that *I'll be Home*, and the peaches and cream girl, Doris Day, proclaiming that *Que Sera Sera*, which means, Whatever will be, will be.

In the cinemas the music continued with the release of *High Society*, music by Cole Porter, starring Bing Crosby and the one and only, Louis Armstrong. But, good as that was, I have to say that my favourite musical film from that time is Rodgers and Hammerstein's *Carousel* starring Gordon McRae (a much-underrated singer in my opinion) and Shirley Jones.

Mid-1950s Entertainment

One of the most popular television programmes around this time was *What's My Line?* where a panel of four celebrities had to work out what the job was of an ordinary member of the public who gave them a clue by demonstrating a brief piece of mime relating to their job. The panel would then ask a series of questions. If any of their guesses received a negative answer from the visitor, the chairman of the panel would turn over a card displaying the word 'No'. The panel were only allowed ten No's and if they hadn't worked out the job by then, the guest was deemed the winner. Some of the panel members I remember included a well-loved and brilliant magician named David Nixon, a very smart and polished lady, Isobel Barnett, and ex-policeman, Gilbert Harding, who made a name for himself due to his rather abrupt manner when questioning the guests. Fortunately, his impatience was somewhat tempered by the last member of the panel, Barbara Kelly, another smart, attractive lady, who had left Canada in 1949 to live in Britain with her husband, Bernard Braden.

The Bradens, both born in Vancouver, quickly made a good impression with the British public. Bernard Braden was a very talented writer and actor. It wasn't long before their natural, easy-going charm, coupled with their Canadian accents, were noticed by the BBC, which resulted in a series entitled *Breakfast with Braden* and was later followed by *Bedtime with Braden*. Barbara Kelly also appeared in these very popular shows which were accompanied by Nat Temple and his Orchestra.

There was much interest in September 1955 when ITV (Independent Television) first came to our television screens. This was a commercial television company who, in direct contrast to the BBC, received the money to make their programmes from companies who were advertising their products on this new channel. Gibbs SR toothpaste went into the history books as being the very first product to be advertised on British television via ITV.

Two adverts which I remember became very popular were for Mars Bars, who informed us that, A Mars a day helps you work, rest and play, and Murray Mints, with the catchy phrase; Murray Mints, Murray Mints, the too good to hurry mints. There were doubts and some consternation from many people who worried that advertising on television would demean the quality of the programmes but, as time passed, we all got accustomed to them, in fact, many people often considered the adverts to be better than the programmes!

The BBC, in an attempt to woo audiences away from ITV's big opening night, let it be known that they were going to 'kill off' Grace Archer – a character from their long running radio serial *The Archers* but it was to no avail, Independent Television had arrived and nothing would ever be quite the same again.

The European Union

In 1957, politicians from France, West Germany, Italy, Belgium, Holland and Luxembourg met in Rome and signed the Treaty of Rome. This treaty encompassed what was also called the Common Market/European Economic Community (EEC) and was the forerunner of what eventually became the European Union (EU). This historic document was followed by five more in later years, each one containing many adaptations and new ideas, but all with one basic aim behind them which was to bring all the European countries together to work for the common good as a Union of Nations or the United States of Europe, as many called them. This Common Market of trading partners was designed to make it easier and cheaper by eliminating much of the time wasted dealing with the red tape involved in exporting and importing to each other. Naturally, many of us thought it sounded a sensible idea, so our government of the time signed Britain up.

With the passing of the years and more treaties written into the constitution, we ended up with a European Parliament hell bent on creating a United States of Europe – this meant that all member countries would cease to make their own rules of self-government and therefore would be subservient to new rules inflicted on them by a European Parliament, made up of unelected politicians from any of the eligible European member countries. This concept that 'one cap fits all' was considered by many people as completely misguided and unrealistic.

I remember wondering how on earth unelected foreign politicians could make decisions which might have a disastrous effect on a small village or community in Britain. Equally, why should we in Britain impose our views on other countries as to how they run their own affairs?

Jumping ahead here, I must tell you that this state of affairs continued for many years afterwards, until the whole European Union fiasco climaxed in 2016 when the then UK Prime Minister, David Cameron, announced a referendum on 23rd June that year, when the British people would have a free vote as to whether the UK remained a member of the European Union, or left it. We were promised that whatever the result of this historic vote, the decision of the people would be carried out. After a bitter struggle throughout the country, the final result was that 51.9% of the people voted to leave and 48.1% to remain. This decision surprised many people and thousands found it hard, or even impossible in many cases, to accept. Some who voted for Britain to remain within the EU claimed the opposition didn't understand what they were doing and demanded a second referendum, whereas leavers retaliated by saying the remainers should accept the decision of the majority in what was, after all, a democratic vote. A new word, Brexit, entered the vocabulary. By this time, David Cameron resigned as Prime Minister and Theresa May took over the role. It's interesting to note that Theresa May herself voted to remain but, all credit to her, in a speech she made after the referendum result, she famously assured the country that, as far as she was concerned, Brexit means Brexit. From that moment in time, rightly or wrongly, she worked tirelessly towards achieving that goal. It has been an almighty struggle with arguments and disagreements from not only the European politicians in Brussels and the Labour party in Britain, but also amongst her own Conservative party members in Parliament.

The UK finally left the EU on 31st January 2020.

Chapter 12

Family Ties

The Greatest Loss

Tragedy struck our family in January 1956 when my mother suffered a recurrence of her cancer, which had first been diagnosed in 1947. Once again, my father's two sisters moved in with us to help nurse her, but it was to no avail, and Mum was again admitted to hospital. After more diagnosis we were given the sad news that there was nothing more they could do and she was brought home where she died on 19th January 1956, aged 60. Although, by this time, we were all prepared for the inevitable ending, it was still hard to come to terms with the reality of the loss.

My mother and father had known each other for 41 years and been married for 37, and even though Dad had survived all the horrors of trench warfare during the First World War, seeing comrades blown to pieces and endured his own physical and mental scars, he described the loss of his wife as the most shattering experience he had ever had. To him, Mum was the finest wife and mother that any man could have.

My brothers and sister would agree with that heartfelt appraisal, we would extend it by saying Mum and Dad were the best parents any child could have.

I was 25 years old when Mum died and it's true to say that as I got older, I realised more and more what a debt we all owed her. At the outbreak of the First World War in 1914, she watched Dad join the thousands of patriotic young men who proudly signed up to the army and marched off to serve their country. Of course, no one knew then the unbelievable hell which awaited them in the battlefields and trenches on the Western Front. Although this madness finished in 1918, Dad didn't return home until the following year. Thankfully, he was physically intact, but mentally scarred by the carnage he had witnessed during those years. Although the horrific memories he had lay mainly dormant within his subconscious mind for the rest of his life, there were times when Dad would have nightmares and scream out in terror. All of us children would also be woken by this and, particularly the younger ones, would be somewhat frightened by these sudden outbursts of unbridled horror, but thankfully Mum was always there to calm Dad's fears and soothe his troubled mind.

Throughout their marriage Mum was always supportive of Dad. Whether it was throughout the duration of the First World War or Dad's meeting with T.E. Lawrence and printing Lawrence's masterpiece *Seven Pillars of Wisdom*, Mum was always there sharing these events with him. Likewise, when Dad was doubtful about accepting the offer of pressman at the Gregynog Press in Wales, it was Mum who resolved the issue by suggesting she would stay in London with us children while Dad worked a three-month trial. The trial period was successful, and so Dad accepted the offer and the family made the move.

This whole area of Wales was, for them, a completely different environment, one which offered green fields, beautiful countryside, tranquillity and clean air where birds sang freely, unlike in smoky, polluted London. But once again it was Mum who was the lynchpin during this period, providing Dad with love and support and not only looking after Bert, Lily and Bernard, but also the two new additions, David and me, who arrived during our time in Wales.

During the Second World War, like many others, Dad and Mum did their share to help on the Home Front. Dad became an ARP (Air Raid Precaution) Warden and, like many other women, Mum responded to the call to help the war effort by working in a factory which made radio parts. So, not only did she cope with feeding Dad and the three of her children at home during this time, despite the food rationing, she also found time to work in the factory, as well as do the hundred and one other things that mothers do for their families. On top of all of that, she had the inner worry of the absence of her two eldest children being drafted into the armed forces. Even when the war finished and both Bert and Lily returned home safely, she still had to face more worry when, in 1947, Bernard was sent to Palestine when the Palestinian war with Israel broke out.

Throughout her life, Mum suffered a lot with dermatitis and yet somehow managed to rise above it, showing great courage, stoicism and fortitude. Being the youngest and last of her children to leave home I, along with my father, witnessed her suffering and pain many times and it hurt us to see it. There were occasions when Mum would be so bad that I would offer to stay in to keep Dad company and help him with Mum, instead of going out with friends but, whilst thanking me for offering, both of them would always insist that I go out and enjoy myself. I think the truth was that Mum was too ill to worry too much and Dad didn't want me to see Mum's pain.

There was one little touch on the day of Mum's funeral which I've always remembered. As the hearse and car procession made its way along the Greenford Road to the cemetery, we passed a man waiting at a bus stop. As we passed him, he quickly removed his hat and bowed his head. I've often thought that this man, a complete stranger to us, will never know what his simple act of respect meant to us.

Finally, I have to say that one of the saddest aspects of Mum dying so young is that, because I had met and married my wife, Kathy, two years after Mum's passing, they never had the chance of meeting each other. Whilst our two sons, Chris and Martin, remember my dad with affection, they also were denied the love, influence and memories they could have shared with Mum.

Two Aunties

Getting through the months following my mother's death were helped in no small way by the support given, once again, by my father's two sisters, Lily and Kate. In addition to Auntie Lily being a member of the St John

Ambulance Brigade, she also loved cooking, so Dad and I had no worries on that score. I remember doing the shopping for Auntie Lily and when she wanted me to get some lamb at the butchers, she always insisted I must ask for 'half a shoulder of lamb, blade end'. What delicious meals she produced, irrespective of which end of the animal she cooked for us! She also made the most delicious egg custard tart, one of my favourites. She was a gentle lady who had two interests in life. The first was being a member of St John Ambulance Brigade. She was often sent to football matches or other public events, ready to administer any medical help. She made us laugh when she came home after one event a little dissatisfied because her nursing skills were not required that particular night, as no one had been injured! Conversely, another time she would exclaim the evening event was, "Good tonight, lots of casualties!" Her second love was cooking and she liked nothing better than being in the kitchen. I remember her conjuring up delicious meals whilst happily chattering away to herself. She had never married and, having worked in service for many years, she considered men to be the masters in the house. This attitude was quite common at that time but has, rightly, since changed due to the long campaigns for women's rights (although this had no effect on Auntie Lily!). As far as she was concerned, she had a duty to provide Dad and I with meals fit for a man, nothing less would do.

Auntie Kate had a completely different persona. She had style and presence, and was very warm-hearted with an easy-going manner. Dad and I and the rest of the family all agreed that we couldn't have had anyone better than these two wonderful ladies to help us all through the trauma of losing Mum. We were also extremely lucky to have my eldest brother Bert and his wife Ethel still living in Greenford and therefore always on hand. My sister Lily and husband Jack were also nearby in South Ruislip. Bernard and David and their wives were further away, but they all gave their support by visiting us and keeping in touch via the telephone.

Every Sunday, my father, along with two neighbours, Lou and Harry, would toddle off to the local Red Lion pub in Greenford for a well-earned pint or three. When Dad returned suitably replenished, he would sit down with his two sisters to attack the lovely Sunday roast dinner (especially if it was the blade end of half a shoulder of lamb) lovingly prepared by Auntie Lily. As this weekly ritual usually didn't start until about 2pm, Auntie Lily would serve my meal earlier, which meant by the time Dad and his sisters sat down to eat I would have finished mine and would be sitting relaxing and listening to their conversation at the table. I remember these occasions with great fondness. Many times, Dad would be holding forth on some subject close to his heart, probably politics. Emboldened by the amber nectar, these weekly *tête-à-têtes* would, at times, be quite hilarious as Auntie Kate, being staunchly of the Conservative persuasion, would differ from Dad's Labour viewpoint and a friendly argument would develop. Throughout these political discussions Auntie Lily would usually get the wrong end of the stick and the two combatants would stop their debate and try to explain their respective points to her, without much success. Meanwhile, I was doubled up with laughter listening to this pantomime, but thankfully it always ended up amicably and the three of them would sleep it off for the next hour or two, only for the whole thing to be repeated the following Sunday.

Dad continued his life as a printer, working for Walter Phillips at his works in Perivale, a daily bicycle journey that Dad made in all weathers. I remember some stormy nights he would arrive home windswept and soaked from the torrential rain he had battled through. Those occasions are reminiscent of the night I was born, when Dad faced similar atrocious weather conditions. Although there were some differences cycling along the well-lit dual carriageway cycle lane from Perivale to Greenford, accompanied by cars and lorries, from the dark, lonely and deserted lanes of Bettws, which were a world away.

The New City Jazzmen

After the Second World War, there was an urgent need for the government to build more houses to replace the loss of so many due to the Blitz, which had left thousands of people homeless, particularly in London. It was decided that certain areas of the country would be developed as designated new towns. Stevenage in Hertfordshire and Harlow in Essex were two such new towns. Another was Crawley in West Sussex. At this time my brother Bernard and his wife Joan were living in a flat in Greenford, and they decided to upgrade and move to Crawley where they bought one of these new houses. They quickly settled in and it wasn't long before Bernard, much to his delight, saw an advert for a trumpet player needed to join a trad band based in Crawley.

Although Crawley was, and still is, a town, it was decided that the band would use some poetic licence and so *The New City Jazzmen* were formed. They were the first band to play at the Crawley Bandstand. This was a big success with the Saturday shoppers and was repeated many times. The band's popularity quickly grew and they were in great demand, performing at weddings, anniversary and birthday parties, as well as corporate functions all over the Sussex and Surrey areas. LP records and CDs were made, copies of which I still have, and they were featured and played on the BBC's Jazz Club. Their success and popularity was to last for the next 54 years, ending on the 15th December 2011 when they played, appropriately, their last gig at the Crawley Bandstand. Although it was a dark and cold December night, people still turned out to hear them. It was also fitting that one of the numbers they played on that final concert was Louis Armstrong's *What a Wonderful World*. The band brought so much pleasure to devotees of trad jazz and their music can still be enjoyed on the internet, a search of *The New City Jazzmen Crawley* brings up a few videos to be enjoyed.

Unfortunately, on 19th June 2018, my brother Bernard died peacefully in a Crawley nursing home aged 90. He and I looked alike, thought alike, shared the same sense of humour and love of both trad jazz and writing. I will be for ever grateful to him for introducing me to trad jazz, which both influenced me and brought much enjoyment to my life.

Chapter 13

A Turn for the Nurse

Learning to Dance

During this period of my life, around 1958, although I had enjoyed a few dates during my RAF days and afterwards, I grew a bit lonely and restless at home with just Dad. This became more apparent when my friend Graeme married and moved away. So, I decided that I should give the fairer sex another chance to renew their acquaintances with me! What better way to do so than to go dancing? The only problem with that was that I couldn't dance. I loved to watch the likes of Fred Astaire and Gene Kelly, but my efforts on the dance floor were more like Gene Astaire and Fred Kelly!

Anyway, undeterred, off I went to a dance studio in nearby Ealing to have a few lessons in the noble art of Terpsichore. In those days, there was a man called Victor Silvester who had been a world champion dancer in his earlier days but went on to teach dancing and formed his own orchestra. He was well-known for only playing strict tempo dance music. When teaching, he would give timing guidance in relation to the steps of the dance, for instance, if the dance was a quickstep, he would instruct the pupil by repeating saying, "Slow, slow, quick quick, slow." This method of teaching was adopted by most dance teachers, including mine. She would play 78rpm (revs per minute) shellac 10-inch gramophone records of the Victor Silvester Orchestra playing a strict tempo dance melody. I started by learning how to do a waltz followed by the foxtrot and then the quickstep. Eventually, I became reasonably proficient and felt that I was ready to demonstrate my new-found skill to the public. Whether they were ready for me is another question!

As luck would have it, one day whilst shopping in Greenford, I bumped into an old school friend of mine, who not only went dancing every Saturday evening, but also had a car and invited me to join him. So, come the next Saturday, Len and I, dressed up to the nines, drove over to Chelsea Town Hall. The place was packed with men and women waltzing, quickstepping, foxtrotting, shuffling around, and trying not to trip over their own feet or kick their partners. It wasn't long before Len found a partner and off he went, gliding around the dance floor whilst I stood, nonchalantly looking around, seeking out someone attractive to approach.

My planned strategy was that because the waltz was the easiest dance to do, I would wait until the band played a waltz before approaching a lady to utter the phrase, "May I have this dance please?"

Eventually, I was lucky and found someone who was willing to take a chance with me on the dance floor.

As we took up our positions to commence the dance, I thought it only right that I should give the poor girl some advance warning of what was to come by saying, "I'm not very good at this." This was accepted with a smile of encouragement and an assurance not to worry. So, with some trepidation on both sides, off we went with the waltz sequence of steps: one-two-three, one-two-three, etc. After the usual introductions of exchanging names, it was considered mandatory to ask your partner, "Do you come here often?" Goodness knows what would have happened if the girl had replied, "Yes, but I won't anymore!" Fortunately, she didn't say that, and we both survived without any injuries or embarrassment. Because all of this happened so many years ago, I cannot recall exactly what happened for the rest of the evening. Suffice to say that Len and I had a drink or two before climbing into Len's car and heading back to Greenford. My first venture into 'tripping the light fantastic' in public may not have been fantastic, but at least I didn't do any tripping. My efforts were considered good enough to try again and, thanks to Len and his car, I continued showing off my dancing prowess, visiting other local dance venues on more Saturday nights.

The Night My Life Changed

Although I usually went dancing on Saturday evenings, it happened that on Friday 13th June 1958, for some reason which I can't recall, Len and I decided we'd have a change of venue and grace the Hammersmith Palais with our presence. This Mecca of dancing, which opened in 1919 and closed in 2007, was a very large, plush venue which kept open throughout the London Blitz and was very popular with many of the armed forces as well as civilians. Band leaders such as Joe Loss, Ken Macintosh and Phil Tate were three of the musicians who brought their orchestras to the Palais, much to the delight of the appreciative dancers.

Well, now we all know that Friday the 13th is considered by many to be unlucky, but as it turned out, that old adage could not have been any further from the truth. Whether it was fate or destiny, call it what you like, this was the day I met the person who was to change my life for ever.

After I had loosened up a little with a few twirls around the floor, I spotted her – a slim, dark-haired, pretty girl, standing all alone watching the other dancers gliding past. Fortunately for me the dance was a waltz, so without hesitation I boldly approached her and said, "May I have this dance please?" She smiled at me and much to my delight said, "Yes." As we stepped onto the shiny dance floor, I warned her of the possible disaster awaiting her by letting her know I wasn't very good, but more delight, and relief, came when she replied that she wasn't very good either.

Now that the barriers were broken, we glided into the one-two-three, one-two-three waltz steps to the manner born and, thankfully, without treading on each other's toes or banging into anyone else! She told me that her name was Kathleen, and she was an SRN (state registered nurse). Having completed her basic nurse's training at Burton-on-Trent, she was now doing part one of her midwifery course at the famous and nearby Queen Charlotte's Hospital.

We survived that first dance intact, but as neither of us were very good dancers, we bided our time awaiting the next waltz to come around. I think we had one or two quicksteps and a foxtrot (which was just a shuffle around for us), but if a jive, tango or a samba were announced, that was our que to steal quietly away for a rest and a drink. I remember it was the Phil Tate Orchestra supplying the music that evening. Once we'd found a quiet table, we rested and had a long talk (or perhaps that should be, we had a long *tête-à-tête* making tentative attempts to learn more about each other).

When the evening came to an end, I found Len and told him I wouldn't be accompanying him in his car back to Greenford. He wished me luck and I escorted Kathleen, who by this time I was calling Kathy (which I preferred and to which she didn't object), back to the nurse's home at Queen Charlotte's Hospital. We said goodnight but not before I found out when her next off-duty day would be and arranged a date to see her again accordingly. With a light heart, I was dancing on air as I quickstepped my way to Shepherd's Bush tube station and caught the train back to Greenford. I went to bed that night a happy man, eagerly looking forward to seeing Kathy the following week.

Over the Rainbow

The following week came, as they have a habit of doing, followed by many more weeks, and each one saw me arriving at Queen Charlotte's Hospital and taking Kathy out. We would often take a stroll along the towpath of the Thames at Hammersmith, usually ending up in one of the Wimpey cafes for a coffee and a hamburger or two. Naturally, during this time we were getting to know each other and liking what we saw more and more.

As our friendship grew it was inevitable that the time would come to introduce Kathy to my dad back home in Greenford. I spoke to Dad about it and he said, "Why don't you bring her home one Sunday and we'll put on a tea for her?" So, when Kathy next had a Sunday off duty, I brought her home to meet Dad. The meeting and having tea together helped to ease any apprehension or nervousness on either side. As it was, they got on fine and I had good feedback from them both. As the weeks passed and our relationship grew even stronger, I took Kathy to meet the rest of my family who also welcomed her with the same ease and kindness shown by my dad.

In August 1958 we managed to get a week's holiday together when we went to Butlin's holiday camp in Clacton-on-Sea. The weather was fine, and we thoroughly enjoyed this new adventure. Just to be together, away from my daily commute and work in London and Kathy enjoying a break from her midwifery lessons, gave us the chance to completely relax and enjoy some of the activates on offer at the camp. We hired a three-wheel bicycle and had a good laugh cycling along the promenade with the wind in our hair and not a care in the world. We also enjoyed the swimming pool in the camp and, of course, we just had to parade our dancing prowess on the dance floor.

A little later in our relationship, we arranged for me to meet Kathy's mother who lived in Lilleshall, Shropshire (her father had died in 1957). I travelled up by train and had the pleasure of meeting her mother who was one of the nicest ladies I, or anyone else, could wish to meet. At the time of her father's death, Kathy was undergoing her nursing training at Burton-on-Trent and living in the nurses' quarters. Whereas her mother, two brothers and sister were living in a house which went with her father's job in Great Gate, near Uttoxeter, Staffordshire. Unfortunately, because of her father's passing, her mother and siblings were forced to leave the house and find alternative accommodation. Fortunately, Kathy's eldest brother, Peter, obtained a job on a farm in Lilleshall, Shropshire, and, once again, the job also included a cottage for the family.

As time went by our relationship continued getting stronger. I remember one day Kathy and I were listening to a record of Judy Garland singing her biggest hit *Over the Rainbow*. As we both loved it very much it became 'our song'. Whenever we hear it, we are reminded of that day in my dad's house when we wished upon a star and how it all came true for us on 27th December 1958 when we were married at Greenford Methodist church. Because Kathy's father had died the year before, her eldest brother, Peter, took his place and walked her down the aisle. My brother David acted as my best man. As we couldn't afford a big expensive honeymoon, we settled for a weekend in the Regent Palace Hotel in London.

Now, as I write this, over 60 years have passed since our wedding day. We celebrated our Diamond wedding anniversary by taking a 12-day trip on the P&O cruise liner ship *Oceana*, visiting Madeira, the Canary Islands and Lisbon. We sailed from Southampton on 17th December which, due to that being my birthday, added another dimension to the happy event. We were also invited to join the captain and his officers to have a champagne breakfast on the morning of the 27th December but, unfortunately, by this time Kathy had gone down with a nasty cold and was in no fit state to leave the cabin to attend.

We decided that I should go and explain and discuss this unfortunate turn of events with the captain. He and his officers were very sympathetic and understanding about the situation, but it was agreed that for Kathy to attend the function would pose too great a risk of passing germs around the ship. As a compromise, the captain kindly arranged for a selection of foods from the breakfast menu, plus the champagne and a beautifully iced cake suitably inscribed with words of celebration befitting a Diamond wedding occasion, to be delivered to our cabin.

Just before I left the captain to return to Kathy, I was asked to stand alongside him and hold up an envelope he had just presented to me. The envelope contained a card of congratulations from Her Majesty Queen Elizabeth II to Kathy and I on reaching our Diamond wedding anniversary, and the ship's photographer was there waiting to record this happy scene for us. This act of acknowledgment by the Queen is something she does for all UK couples upon reaching this milestone, providing the official department in Buckingham Palace receives prior notification supplying all the necessary details.

About 15 minutes after I returned to our cabin, the breakfast trolley arrived and Kathy and I were able to relax and sample some of the delights upon it. We left the champagne for a later date and, after I had sampled some of the iced cake, I asked for the remainder to be shared amongst the waiters attending us at our table in the dining room.

Who would have thought that 60 years from our wedding day on 27th December 1958 we would be not only still alive, but celebrating our Diamond wedding anniversary at sea on a cruise liner in the Mediterranean?

So, bearing all that in mind, it is only fitting to recall three of the biggest hit songs of 1958, which were the Everly Brothers singing *All I Have to Do is Dream* (which is what I was doing in those days back in 1958), Connie Francis singing *Who's Sorry Now?* – that definitely wasn't me because, as one of my all-time favourite singers, Perry Como, sang that year, those heady days were, for me, wonderful *Magic Moments*. So, to sum it up, my family, like me, were all glad I had gone to that dance on Friday 13th June 1958 and ended up taking a 'turn for the nurse'.

Early Married Life

In 1959, Kathy and I were very lucky to start our married life by accepting the offer of having two rooms in my dad's house in Wedmore Road. This same act of kindness had been done twice before, firstly, when my sister Lily and her husband Jack moved in after they married and stayed until they eventually found their own property in nearby Ruislip, then my brother David and his wife Doreen moved in after their marriage in 1952. They followed the same pattern as Lily and Jack and only moved out when they found a flat, or what was in those days called a maisonette, in Isleworth, Middlesex.

Whilst Kathy was still in her midwifery training at Queen Charlotte's and living in the nurses' quarters, I was still living with Dad, but it wasn't long before she successfully completed her training and was able to join me in Wedmore Road. We were very happy as we settled into our new environment thanks to Dad. We were very grateful to him for giving us this start which enabled us to dream that one day, like both Lily and David, would be in a position to buy our own property.

Sharing with Dad was easy and there was a fortuitous element to it which benefited us all. This was that, due to the fact I worked shift hours, there were many evenings when I didn't get home until 10 or 10.30pm, and rather than Kathy being on her own, Dad would always invite her into his sitting room where they watched television together, thus providing company for each other.

It wasn't long before Kathy got a job nursing at King Edward's Hospital in nearby Ealing, and we were able to add a few more 'pennies' to our income. I remember we would visit the shops in West Ealing, looking wistfully through the windows at the many items on sale. We worked, saved and managed to buy a three-piece suite (two armchairs and a sofa) for our lounge. This 'luxury' cost us the princely sum of £45, which was a lot of money to us in 1959. In due course, other items were added as we put our stamp onto our room. Married life was getting better all the time and it was to get even better when, on 24th October that year, another great life-changing event occurred. It was when our first child, a boy, was born. Not surprisingly, he was born in Queen Charlotte's Hospital and we named him Christopher John.

Becoming parents was a wonderful experience and we embraced it with love and gratitude. I was so glad that Kathy already had the natural loving instincts of a mother (which she'd inherited from her own mother) and this attribute, combined with her common sense and nursing training, meant I just had to watch, learn and provide love and all the support required to mother and child, which I was naturally glad to do.

My father was also thrilled to not only have another grandchild, his sixth, but this child, being a boy, meant he would carry on the Hodgson name. This sentiment was also shared by my three brothers, Bert, Bernard and David, and my sister, Lily. Dad kindly helped us with the cost of buying a pram for Chris. It was a lovely experience for us to put Chris into this gleaming white chariot and proudly walk down the street, showing him off to all the neighbours.

Events of the Late-1950s

Meanwhile, whilst we were preoccupied with our lives, there were other events which were occurring in the UK at this time.

I shall never forget the evening of 6th February 1958. I was at work in London when the news came through that the plane carrying the Manchester United football team had crashed on a snow-covered runway at Munich Airport in Germany. The team were returning from playing a cup tie match in Belgrade which, at that time, was in Yugoslavia. After refuelling at Munich, the plane bound for Britain crashed on take-off. Seven of the young 'Busby Babes' (named after their manager, Matt Busby) were killed. Another one, Duncan Edwards, was so badly injured that he died 15 days later. Matt Busby was also badly injured and spent a long time in hospital in Munich, as did the wonderful player Bobby Charlton – one of the best players England ever produced.

Despite this tragedy, Manchester United, under deputy manager Jimmy Murphy, were able to blend together a team good enough to reach the FA Cup final four months later in May 1958. The emotion felt by everyone that day at Wembley Stadium as the team walked out to face their opponents, Bolton Wanderers, was heart-rendering. Unfortunately, a storybook ending wasn't to be as Bolton beat them comfortably by two goals to nil.

A completely different event happened in the same year when the government announced that because Mayfair was deemed to be the most affluent area in the country, it would be the first area to have parking meters installed.

Other new events which happened in 1958 included the opening of Britain's first planetarium in London on 21st March. Another first for the country was the opening of the eight-mile-long Preston bypass in Lancashire, which was opened by then Prime Minister, Harold Macmillan, who was driven along a four-mile stretch of our first motorway. Further history occurred in the April when an act was passed allowing women to sit in the House of Lords. Another big event was the Campaign for Nuclear Disarmament forming and we witnessed its strength of feeling when over 3,000 protesters marched to the Nuclear Establishment at Aldermaston in Berkshire. This was the first of many similar marches which involved the police fighting to control disparate crowds of protesters, many of them women, venting their feelings.

Talking of unrest, there were terrible race riots in the Notting Hill area of London in September 1958. On a brighter note, British Overseas Airways Corporation (BOAC) launched the first transatlantic jet service, and millions throughout the country watched the first televised State Opening of Parliament. Also, Her Majesty The Queen made history when she dialled the first trunk call on the new do-it-yourself telephone system. The call she made was from Bristol to Edinburgh, and after a brief talk with the city's Lord Provost, she then threw a switch which linked 18,000 Bristol subscribers to the new service.

In the world of sport, the 1958 Grand National was
won by a horse called *Mr What* and the Derby by
Hard Ridden. On the cricket front, Surrey won the
Championship for a record seven successive seasons.
In motorsport Mike Hawthorn became the first Briton
to be crowned Motor Racing Champion of the World.
Unfortunately, his glory was short lived as he sadly died
in a road accident on the A3 near Guilford in Surrey a
few months later. Still on the fast cars scene, the British
Motor Corporation unveiled the Austin Healey Sprite
for the first time. Away from land speed, Donald
Campbell achieved a new water speed record of 248.62
mpg. Over at SW19 (Wimbledon), Australian Ashley
Cooper beat his compatriot Neale Fraser to win the
Men's Tennis Championship, whilst American Althea
Gibson beat our own British girl from Torquay, Angela
Mortimer, to take the ladies' title. Meanwhile, up at
Lytham St Anne's, Aussie star Peter Thomson won
the Open golf tournament for the fourth time. It is
interesting to note that the second, third and fourth
players behind Thomson were all from the UK, namely
Dave Thomas from Wales, Christy O'Connor Snr from
Northern Ireland, and Eric Brown from Scotland.

In the entertainment world, Hollywood bestowed three
Oscars on the wonderful David Lean film, *The Bridge
on the River Kwai*. Another equally successful film was
My Fair Lady, a musical based on a story written by
George Bernard Shaw called *Pygmalion,* which starred
Rex Harrison, Audrey Hepburn and Stanley Holloway.

The Royal Variety Show had a plethora of stars
performing that year, such as Julie Andrews, Rex

Harrison, Stanley Holloway, Norman Wisdom, Harry Secombe, Bruce Forsyth, Tony Hancock, Roy Castle, Max Bygraves, The Beverley Sisters, Frankie Vaughan, Harry Worth, Hattie Jacques, David Nixon and American singers Pat Boone and Eartha Kitt.

The country suffered a very severe frost in January 1959, which caused the newly opened Preston Bypass, Britain's first motorway, to be closed whilst repairs were carried out. Even worse was to come at the end of the month, when the whole transport system throughout Britain was in utter chaos as the worst winter fog since 1952 enveloped the country, causing widespread disruption.

An historical event occurred when the Jodrell Bank telescope transmitted radio messages to the US via the Moon. Back on Earth, the Queen journeyed to Canada and, along with America's President Eisenhower, inaugurated the St Lawrence Seaway. Barclays Bank became the first British Bank to order the new gadget, a computer. That's when all our troubles started, "Sorry sir, it's a computer error!"

Cinemas throughout Britain were closing at a rapid rate as television took over as the main provider for mass entertainment. In October, the country held a general election when the Conservative Party led by Harold Macmillan won by the massive majority of 365 seats to Labour's 258. The prime minister, with a wonderful example of British understatement, summed up his big victory with the words, "It has gone off rather well." Among the nine new women MPs elected was one Margaret Thatcher, who, 20 years later in 1979, made history as Britain's first female prime minister and served for 11 years and 209 days.

British rule over the island of Cyprus ended after 80 years when an agreement was signed in London handing over independence to the Cypriots, but Britain still retained its two military bases on the island. On a lighter note, the latest rave was the new Transistor radio which only cost £23 and was displayed at the Earl's Court exhibition. In addition to the arrival of the Mini, there was also the Rolls-Royce Phantom V which could be yours for a 'mere' £8,905. I considered buying one but it didn't have one of the new Transistor radios, so I didn't bother!

Reflecting on My Defining Years

At this point in my story, I'd like to tell you that for many years I have considered the 1950s to be what I can only describe as my defining years. The events I encountered, good and, sadly, one tragically bad, were to change my life for ever.

Looking back, it all started in March 1950 when I was called up for National Service in the Royal Air Force. I can truthfully say that I enjoyed my two years of service as they held no worries for me. I was used to mixing with other boys throughout my days with the Boys' Brigade. I was lucky that the BB taught me how to march and perform all the drill movements required in the RAF. I also learnt how to handle a rifle, even becoming a marksman (a requirement thankfully not required in the BB!).

Another difference between these two services were that the boys I mixed with in the BB were mainly local boys I knew, some from the same school as me, whereas the boys (and girls) I met in the RAF were from all corners of the UK, many with different accents, outlooks and upbringings. There is no doubt that experiencing this was a great learning curve and an education in itself.

I am always grateful to the RAF for the training I received in signal communications through my service. The training, knowledge and experience I gained was put to good use when I was demobbed. It eventually gave me a good, rewarding career throughout my 37 years using this knowledge in civilian life. This started in June 1952 when I joined the American Embassy in London. This was an interesting and eye-opening period of my life applying my telegraphic skills with American colleagues, who were very pleasant and generous people.

Whilst I was working at the Embassy, I heard there were similar work openings in the telecommunications field at the Shell Petroleum Company, also in London. In addition, I also learnt that Shell offered a very generous life pension scheme. Whilst I enjoyed my days at the Embassy, I decided to apply to Shell. I was successful in my application and joined Shell in December 1952, staying with them until my retirement in December 1989.

The death of my mother in January 1956 was, alas, a very bittersweet, definitive and heart-breaking moment and one that can never be forgotten. The pain was somewhat eased two years later by meeting Kathy in

June 1958 and marrying her six months later in December 1958. As a result of our liaison, there was the other and wonderful definitive moment when our first child, Chris, was born in October 1959.

So, taking all the experiences, knowledge and advancement I lived through in the 1950s into account, is it any wonder I call this decade 'my defining years'?

Part 4
1960s

Chapter 14

The Swinging Sixties Have Arrived

The Early 1960s

Although I consider the 1950s to be my defining years, the 1960s have gone down in history as the 'Swinging Sixties'. American singer Roger Miller summed it up well with his song *England Swings*, which features the lyrics, 'England swings like a pendulum do'. That swinging feeling quickly spread throughout the country. Starting in London, the fashion industry took off in King's Road in Chelsea, and Carnaby Street. The young men, many with long hair, sideburns and Zapata moustaches, paraded the streets wearing flowered shirts and chiffon scarves, whilst the girls shocked the older generation with their mini skirts. Designer Mary Quant was the queen of fashion, and models Leslie Hornby (known as 'Twiggy' due to her very slim body) and Jean Shrimpton, known as 'The Shrimp', were the icons all the girls and photographers, particularly David Bailey, followed.

All of this new fashion was accompanied by the changing music scene which really exploded with popular groups such as The Hollies and Herman's

Hermits from Manchester, The Animals from Newcastle, The Moody Blues, The Move, and Spencer Davis, all from Birmingham, and the Rolling Stones from London. But without doubt the capital of the music scene was Liverpool, which gave us The Searchers, Gerry and the Pacemakers, Billy J. Kramer, Cilla Black and The Beatles. It really was a time of social revolution in Britain which subsequently had a big impact around the world.

Our First Home

Whilst this new revolution was making headlines, Kathy and I decided that it was time for us to take the plunge to leave Wedmore Road and start looking for our own property. It wasn't long before we found one which looked suitable. It was a two-bedroom mid-terrace house in Bedford Road, Ruislip Gardens. It was priced at £2,750 – a sum which was beyond our means at that time, unless I took out a mortgage. It was fortunate for us that Shell had a mortgage arrangement scheme with the Halifax Building Society whereby Shell employees could obtain a mortgage without having to pay a deposit. This meant that I was able to obtain a 100% mortgage loan for the whole £2,750 asking price of the house. This loan required a repayment of £15 per month, which was a lot of money out of my monthly income at that time. Many of my work colleagues thought it was a bit reckless, but after much financial deliberation on our part, helped by my brother Bernard's advice that it was generally accepted that putting money into bricks and mortar was a good investment, we went ahead and bought our first house.

The layout of this house comprised of two medium-sized bedrooms, a similar size lounge with wood block flooring and patio doors leading out to a back garden which had a lawn with flower borders on either side. The garden was fenced on both sides and at the back there was a paved car parking area which could be accessed from an alleyway to the road. The kitchen was of a reasonable size with a coal/coke burning boiler supplying the hot water and a good-sized larder. The usual sink, cooking facilities and storage cupboards were all there, plus the back door leading out to the garden. To complete the description, there were stairs leading up to the landing and the two bedrooms plus a bathroom and toilet.

Whilst such a house was small and somewhat lacking in luxuries, it was ours and we were very excited and happy to move in. Bedford Road was a long road with many similarly designed houses on it and ours, number 62, was roughly half way down. It was no distance for me to walk down to Ruislip Gardens underground station for my daily commute to work. Shopping facilities were a bus ride away in Ruislip or nearly Ruislip Manor. Likewise, we were also only a short car ride from Greenford and visiting Dad, which was also convenient. We were lucky that our neighbours were pleasant and, fortunately, they also had a baby boy of similar age to Chris. We settled in and gradually when time and finances allowed, started to make some alterations to one or two rooms by decorating and painting. It was a labour of love and very satisfying. Another thing we did was to buy two bicycles, one for Kathy and one for me, to which I fixed a safety seat behind my saddle for Chris to sit on. With a haversack containing some refreshments upon my back and Chris safely strapped into his back seat, the three of us would ride off beyond the blue (sometimes!) horizon. The only downside to this was that sometimes Chris got a little too excited on the back and would kick his shoes off, bringing our convoy to a grinding halt for the necessary replacement of said shoes.

A New Arrival

In 1962, another life-changing event happened when, in May, Kathy went into Queen Charlotte's Hospital once again and on Saturday 5th she had another baby boy, who we named Martin Charles. It so happened that it was the FA Cup final on that day, and my cup runneth over when my team, Tottenham Hotspur, beat Burnley 3-1. What a wonderful and unforgettable day that was. I'm pleased to say that Martin eventually took an interest in football and followed my lead by also supporting Spurs.

Wheels in Motion (Just)

Our family was now complete with two lovely, healthy sons and life moved on. We ended our cycling days later that year when my brother Bert rang me to tell me his neighbour was selling his car and Bert wondered if I might be interested in buying it. We managed to scrape together the £27.50 asking price and purchased our first car, a classic six-cylinder 1937 Lanchester 14 hp two-tone grey/blue saloon, with real leather seats, a running board on each side of the body, and a spare wheel encased in a cover attached to the back above an iron grid, which folded down so a suitcase or two could be attached with leather straps. Another feature was a small cog wheel on the dashboard, to which a winding handle was attached. By turning this handle the windscreen would open from the bottom outwards, thus letting in fresh air which was a boom on a very hot summer's day.

The biggest feature of this quality car was the method of driving it. It had what was called a 'pre-selector gearbox'. There was a gear lever on the steering column showing the choices of N for Neutral, D for Drive, 1 for first gear, 2 for second gear and 3 for third gear, with R for reverse. It didn't have the normal clutch foot pedal to press down and then slowly release to engage your selected gear. Instead, there was a foot pedal, called the gear engaging pedal. The method used to drive the car was to pull the gear lever down to the required gear (first gear to get going!) and press the gear engaging foot pedal right down to the floor and immediately release it – you were then in first gear but nothing further happened until you selected D for drive, and released the hand brake, whereupon the car silently glided. Once you were on the move, you pulled gear lever to 2, but you weren't in second gear until you depressed and released the gear engaging foot pedal again. This method of selecting the required gear and operating the foot engaging pedal in and out was all you had to do to drive. It was easy and effective, and although it took some time for me to adjust to this method, I eventually mastered it. The car was smooth and comfortable and served us well throughout the years 1962 and 1963. The only drawback was that it did swallow up the petrol and oil too much, so after those two years we decided we couldn't afford to keep it any longer.

Fortunately for us, my neighbour admired it and was willing to buy it from me. We agreed upon a price of £15 and the deal was done. Now, the big snag for my neighbour was that he couldn't drive. Unlike me, he didn't have a garage to house the car so I drove it around to his back garden and parked it there for him. Although he couldn't drive, he thought it prudent to run the engine once a week to 'warm it up a bit'. This became a ritual and every Sunday we saw him climb into this beautiful car wearing a pair of large leather gloves, and he would start her up and just sit there, letting the engine idle as he imagined he was driving through the leafy lanes on a warm summer's day being admired by other drivers. I told him that this didn't do the engine any good but he wouldn't listen, so I gave up. As the winter months were fast approaching, I also advised him to put some anti-freeze into the car, but he just smiled and didn't bother, so I let him carry on in his Walter Mitty dream world.

The end result was inevitable, he ruined the engine and the lack of anti-freeze cracked the block. As he couldn't afford to pay for any repairs, he was forced to get a couple of men to come around to break up the whole car. It was very sad to see the desecration of a lovely classic car by these two men as they took their sledge hammers and systematically smashed the windscreen, before moving on to the body work. The whole vehicle was smashed up and then thrown onto their lorry as scrap and taken away for disposal.

Our time in our first house came to an end in 1965 when we decided to move from Ruislip to a newly built three-bedroom semi-detached house in Church Crookham, near Fleet in Hampshire. It is worth recording that my brother Bernard was right in his advice to us about investing in property, because after our five happy years living in Ruislip, the house we paid £2,750 for in 1960 was sold for £4,750, making a profit of £2,000, which was a lot of money to us.

Britain Says Goodbye, and Defining Events

The date 24th January 1965 brought the sad, but not unexpected news, of the death of Sir Winston Churchill, aged 90. The country and much of the free world mourned his passing. For three days his coffin lay in state at Westminster Hall in the heart of the Houses of Parliament. Hundreds of thousands of people filed past, paying their respects. Representatives of 110 nations from around the world attended his funeral service in St Paul's Cathedral. It seemed everyone wanted to honour this colossus and extraordinary man of destiny, whose inspired leadership and defiant bulldog spirit was responsible for the survival of Britain and much of the free world during the dark days of the Second World War. I remember his radio broadcasts when we would all gather around the radio and listen to his mastery of the English language. In spite of Hitler's threats, Churchill's voice and the emotion he put into his words sent a strong surge of patriotic fervour throughout the whole nation. Even France's General De

Gaulle agreed when he said of Churchill, "In the war drama, he was the greatest."

The big sporting occasion of 1966 was England winning the football World Cup (at least it was for all Englishmen, but I'm not so sure for the rest of the countries that make up the United Kingdom!). There was a fright before the tournament started when the actual cup was stolen from Westminster Hall where it was on display. It was found a week later, when a Thames lighterman's dog was spotted tearing at an object wrapped in newspaper. To everyone's surprise and delight, the bundle contained the Jules Rimet trophy, for which 16 countries were preparing to do battle in July.

Battle was the right word for some of the games, too. England's manager, Alf Ramsey (who was later knighted for steering England to victory), referred to some of the Argentine players as 'animals' in the game against England. The whole country, including many women, was drawn into the football fever which spread throughout the land. England eventually went through to the final, and I remember that magical July Saturday at Wembley Stadium well, when England's Captain, Bobby Moore, led the England team out to face Germany. Millions throughout the country were glued to their television sets, willing on their heroes. The match was fiercely fought as you'd expect. Despite some controversy over one of England's goals, the match ended in England winning 4-2.

The names of the English team on that glorious day went into the history books and, even today, there are many old-timers like me who still remember Captain Bobby Moore, the brothers Jack and Bobby Charlton, Gordon Banks, Martin Peters, Nobby Stiles, George Cohen, Ray Wilson, Alan Ball, Roger Hunt, and thankfully, Geoff Hurst, who scored a hat-trick for which he was later awarded a knighthood. It should be noted that Bobby Charlton also received a knighthood for his services to football.

Another reason why I remember the match so well is because our next-door neighbour at the time was a German lady; a very nice, friendly person who had married an Englishman after fleeing from Germany at the end of the Second World War, and settled in England. As she and her husband weren't interested in football at all, Kathy and I watched the match in our house. This enabled me to shout out freely such rallying cries as, "Come on England!" without fear of causing any offence or annoyance to our neighbours.

The 1960s saw many changes throughout the world. For instance, the assassination of American President, John Kennedy, in November 1963, as he was driven in a motorcade through Dallas in Texas, was one of the most-remembered events. I recall the utter shock which reverberated around the world as we watched this horrific murder on our television screens. People still to this day recall what they were doing at that particular moment in time. I, as usual, was at work.

Some significant legal changes happened in Britain in the mid-1960s. In 1965, the death penalty for murder was abolished in England, Scotland and Wales, and in 1967, both homosexuality and abortion were legalised.

History was made in December 1967, when South African surgeon, Dr Christiaan Barnard, performed the first successful heart transplant on another human being. The recipient of this new heart was another South African by the name of Louis Washkansky, who survived the operation and lived for another 18 years.

The year 1968 saw two horrific murders. In April, the leader of the American civil rights movement, Martin Luther King, was murdered in Memphis, Tennessee, and in the following month the late President John F. Kennedy's brother, Robert (Bobby), was murdered in Los Angeles. This came five years after his brother's assassination.

The last year of the decade will forever be remembered as the year when man landed on the Moon for the first time. American astronaut, Neil Armstrong, was the first man to actually step onto the lunar surface, followed by his colleague, astronaut Edward (Buzz) Aldrin. The third member of the crew in this world-shattering event was Michael Collins, who manned the space capsule as it orbited the Moon, whilst Armstrong and Aldrin were examining the planet's surface, taking photographs and recording material which was transmitted down to mission control in Houston, Texas. It really was an awe-inspiring feat of ingenuity, bravery and discovery for the world. There were many people, me included, who couldn't help wondering if these three brave men were going to be successfully returned to Mother Earth.

Thank goodness they were, and the world breathed a gigantic sigh of relief and admiration.

I include these historical facts in my story because I lived through them and, not only can I recall the shock and horror at some of the tragic and evil events which occurred during these periods, but I can also consider how lucky I am to remember some of the wonderful feats performed by many men and women in the fields of medicine and science. We all owe them for their work and dedication which benefits mankind now and in the future.

Chapter 15

Our Life in the 1960s

Commuting in the 1960s

Moving to Fleet brought a slight change to my daily commute to work. From our house in Ruislip Gardens, it was only a five-minute walk to the train station where I caught a Central line tube train and changed at Oxford Circus to the Northern line for my train to Waterloo. But now, because our new house in Church Crookham was over two miles from Fleet station, I used my car (a 1957 Ford Popular) for this daily journey and parked the car in the station car park, for which there was a parking fee. My mode of transport was later changed to cycling. As I had sold my bicycle before the move to Fleet, and not wishing to buy another one, I resorted to visiting the local dump (scrap yard or recycling centre). I found an old but serviceable bike frame, which I painted green, some old mudguards and other necessary bits and pieces which enabled me to assemble a bike myself.

At this point I should tell you that, unlike the frequent London Underground trains which I used from Ruislip to London, the rail service from Fleet to Waterloo in those days was one steam train an hour. When I was on early duty, which was on alternate days, I started work at 8am. This meant that, to allow time for any train delays, and not wanting to be late, I would leave my house at 6.15am to catch the 6.43am train from Fleet, which arrived at Waterloo at 7.30am, thus giving me plenty of time to get to work for my 8am start.

I used to attach my briefcase to a holding rack behind my saddle. Upon arriving at Fleet station, I would dismount, dash onto the platform and park my bike in the covered area reserved for all bicycles. After locking up my bike and removing my briefcase from the back, I would cross over the bridge to the opposite platform to catch the train to Waterloo.

There were some days, particularly in winter, when I might oversleep. This resulted in a mad dash on my trusty steed to the station. With briefcase firmly attached to the rack, my head down and my legs pedalling like pistons, I hurtled along Fleet high street nearly breaking the sound barrier. It's no wonder my bike was known as the 'Green Flash'. Heaven help anyone who crossed my flight path as I raced into the station on one of these days. There was a very helpful porter at Fleet station named Vic who, upon seeing any passenger arriving late and panic-stricken for the London train, would warn the train driver by shouting, "One coming over!" as they dashed across the bridge. I must admit that on those occasions when I was one of the late comers and Vic wasn't on duty, I would copy his warning and shout out, "One coming over" to the driver as I ran across the bridge, down the steps onto the platform and grabbed the handle of the first carriage door I could reach. Complete with briefcase, I would fall into the carriage, receiving somewhat startled and amused looks from some of the other passengers who were 'hiding' behind their morning newspapers.

The cost of an annual season ticket commuting from Fleet to Waterloo was £108. There was no way I could afford a lump sum of that amount on my own but, fortunately, once again, Shell came to the rescue as they did with my mortgage. They had a scheme whereby they supplied the required amount to any employee who couldn't afford the price of a season ticket in one lump sum, which was then paid back in monthly instalments from the employee's salary. As a point of interest, when I retired from Shell in 1989, I believe that the cost of an annual season ticket for the same journey had increased to over £1,300, and now, in 2022, the cost is over £4,300.

During my days of travelling from Fleet to Waterloo, I was sometimes caught up in delays or change of trains. Naturally, it's quite common for train delays to be due to breakdowns, bad weather, shortage of staff, and similar inconveniences, but during the 1960s there was another reason which was more serious and dangerous. This was the IRA (Irish Republican Army) threats of bombs being strategically placed in designated locations, particularly in London, i.e., mainline train stations.

I remember the occasions when, after work, I dashed from my office across York Road into Waterloo station, aiming to catch the 9.12pm train home, only to be confronted by police stopping all passengers boarding trains, because of warnings they had received claiming there were IRA bombs planted somewhere in the station. This could cause a delay of up to an hour, which was inconvenient to say the least.

On the bright side, when travelling from Waterloo station I once had the pleasure of seeing comedian and magician, Tommy Cooper, talking to a porter, and on another occasion, while walking down the platform I passed golfer Peter Allis, who had alighted from the train I was about to board. I could have shouted out 'Fore!' but I didn't. Talking of Peter Allis, some years later I purchased a second-hand golf club, a five iron, in an antique shop in Horncastle, Lincolnshire. On the back of the club head it bore the name Percy Allis, Peter's father (or should I say, par?). I wrote to Peter Allis about my purchase and received a nice polite and friendly reply from him, which was a welcome touch. Peter Allis was a top golfer for many years and eventually went on to become a top BBC golf commentator. His knowledge and experience of the game, coupled with his wonderful and amusing anecdotes gleaned over many years, were passed on to all devotees of golf in his broadcasts.

In February 1963, the whole railway system in Britain was changed dramatically when, due to the loss of money, the Government asked Richard Beeching to leave his high-profile job in ICI (Imperial Chemical Industries) to take on the task of streamlining the whole train network system and making it more profitable.

Beeching undertook this colossal task and reduced one third of the network, achieved by closing hundreds of branch lines, 5,000 miles of track, over 2,000 stations and tens of thousands of jobs. The whole adventure has gone down in our history as a fiasco and a complete financial disaster. Even now, one hears people reflecting back on earlier times and saying things with the train network were fine before Beeching came along and ruined everything.

Another train story worth repeating is to tell you how lucky I was on 12th December 1988, when I was travelling on my usual 6.43am train from Fleet, which arrived at Waterloo on time at 7.30am. I then crossed the road and went into my office in Shell Centre. At about 8.20am, my wife Kathy phoned and was so relieved to hear me answer. The reason for her relief was because she had just heard on the radio that there had been a terrible accident at Clapham Junction station (a station just outside of Waterloo) at around 8.13am. This tragedy has gone down in history as the Clapham Junction accident of 1988. Three trains were involved. One train crashed into the back of another which had stopped at a signal, and then hit an empty train going in the opposite direction. Thirty-five people lost their lives and 70 people had horrific injuries. If I had missed my usual train from Fleet that morning, I would have been on the next one which was one of the three involved in the disaster. No wonder Kathy was worried and, subsequently, so relieved when I answered the phone that morning.

A more eventful train journey of mine happened one morning when I left home at my usual time of 6.15am heading for the 6.43am train. The weather was reasonably warm with a slight wind which accompanied the early morning bird song as I headed off for another day at the office. Due to the wind blowing and knowing that my wide-brimmed hat had a tendency to leave my head, I pulled it down tighter as I pedalled faster to keep my rendezvous with the 6.43am train. Unfortunately, with hat and head down, I had restricted my vision ahead and, before I knew what was happening, there was a loud sound of metal hitting metal as my trusty Green Flash crashed into the back of a parked car on the road outside someone's house. I just didn't see it in time. My bike hit the offside light cluster and broke the glass and bulbs of a red MG sports car. The bike went one way and I went another, whilst my briefcase and hat sought sanctuary somewhere else amidst this scattered heap in the middle of the road. I remember there was a milk delivery van passing by, but the driver only gave me a fleeting glance. I imagined he was thinking, What's this idiot doing at this time of the morning? The final insult was to find that because of my fall onto the road, I had sustained a cut to my trousers just below the knee and a wound to my leg which was now bleeding. I also broke a tooth when I hit the deck which wasn't exactly a laugh.

After picking myself up and making a note of the house number I, in the true spirit of the Royal Air Force, picked up my bike and reassembled the briefcase and hat to their original places. So, with briefcase back on the rack behind the saddle and hat jammed more firmly on my head I remounted the somewhat embarrassed Green Flash and peddled very slowly back home, having decided I was in no fit state to continue my hazardous journey to the station.

As I opened my front door, Kathy appeared at the top of the stairs, surprised at my sudden reappearance back home. When I told her I had run into the back of a car around the corner and in doing so had cut my trousers and leg, which was still bleeding, we both had to laugh a bit at the stupidity of the situation. Chris and Martin, who were just getting ready for school, also enjoyed Dad's little accident! As I was still a little shaken after all this excitement, I decided I couldn't face going to work. I went back to bed and slept for about half an hour to aid recovery. After a good rest I got up and dressed, which included a change of trousers.

Feeling guilty about the damage I'd done, I walked back around the corner to the scene of the crime. As I approached the scene, I saw a man standing by the damaged MG sports car. After ascertaining that he was the owner, I immediately owned up to being the person who had hit his pride and joy. He was most surprised to learn that it was a bicycle which had caused the damage, due to the fact that he had found a small piece of green paint on the road near his car, and assumed it must have been a green car which had caused the damage. He had spent some time walking up and down the road looking for such a car and seeking the owner, but with no result. I assured him that the green paint was from my bike and not someone's car.

After more apologies from me I told him to get the damage fixed and I would pay for it. He accepted my apologies and later that day came to my house to tell me that he had replaced the damaged light cluster on his car. He said he was grateful for my honesty and wanted to repay it and did this by not going to a shop and paying full price for a new light cluster unit, but instead he visited a local car breaker's yard and found a second-hand cluster unit which did the job perfectly well, and, of course, at a much cheaper price. So, it all ended up amicably.

I'm pleased to say the Green Flash, minus a small piece of missing green paint, survived the crash and went on for many more years, flashing its way to and from Fleet station avoiding all vehicles, especially MG sport cars. It was finally retired when its owner hung up his cycle clips in January 1989.

First Family Holiday

When our two boys were young, we took them on various holidays including camping in tents to places such as Littlehampton, Brighton and Weymouth, but our biggest adventure was taking them to Comrie, Perthshire in Scotland. Because I only had a Ford Prefect car at that time, it was decided that it wasn't big enough to carry the four of us, plus a tent and all the paraphernalia for a journey of approximately 450 miles from Crookham to the camping site we'd booked at Comrie. Help came when Kathy's Uncle Phil offered us his metal trailer which hitched onto a towing bar on the back of my car. This trailer had a hinged lockable lid, a spare wheel and a solid water container attached to the back. It was perfect for our needs, so off we trundled to bonnie Scotland, loaded to the brim. I remember many hours later we were travelling over Beatock Summit and along a road in the vicinity of Moffatt, which, in those days, was in Dumfriesshire (later to become Dumfries and Galloway), when a train suddenly appeared running alongside the road we were travelling on. Many of the train passengers were looking out of their windows and waving at Chris and Martin who waved back to them. It was a lovely welcoming moment to Scotland. We still had approximately 90 miles to go to Comrie, but we eventually arrived at our camping site and pitched our tent.

This was our first of many subsequent visits to Scotland and we enjoyed visiting such places as Pitlochry, where we all enjoyed seeing the salmon leaping. We also saw Loch Tummel and admired the scenery from the Queen's View. We went to Loch Tay and Crieff, a town which I believe was used for filming parts of what became a very popular television series called *Dr Finlay's Casebook*. Another trip we did was taking a long car journey out to Braemar. The roads were deserted and we enjoyed the peace and serenity of the area. We stopped for a picnic but, unfortunately, it started to rain. Not to be denied our picnic I opened one of the car's back doors and fixed up a piece of waterproof sheeting, under which Kathy cooked some sausages on a small camping stove. They were delicious and after we were suitably replenished and the rain eased sufficiently, we continued our exploration of the route to Braemar.

The rain we encountered on the journey to Braemar was nothing compared to what was to come later. The sad truth was that on our 14-day holiday in Scotland we had 10 days of rain, some of which was of Biblical proportions. We tried to make the best of it by finding places to take Chris and Martin to escape the rain, but suitable dry places to satisfy our quest weren't so easy to find. I remember sitting in the tent and wistfully saying to Kathy, "What are we doing, sitting here 450 miles from home in a tent with our two young adventure-seeking children, with thunder and lightning all around us and the seemingly never-ending torrential rain lashing down on our newly purchased canvas home?"

Despite the dismal weather, we remember one dry day when the rain took pity on us and stopped. We made the most of it by paying a visit to my sister-in-law Ethel's brother, Bob, and his wife, Nancy, who lived in Hamilton. They made us very welcome and gave us a guided tour of the area which included a visit to the Mausoleum where many of the Duke of Hamilton's family members are buried.

Eventually, the end of the holiday came and it was time for us to dismantle the tent, which, fortunately, had dried out sufficiently for us to pack it into the trailer, hitch the trailer up to the car and commence our 450-mile journey home. We left on a Friday evening with the intention of driving through the night and only stopping for occasional breaks for food and some sleep. To this end, Kathy made up a 'bed' for Chris and Martin in the back of the car and because it was important that I, as the driver, should have a sleep or two to keep us all safe, Kathy and I swapped front seats. By me sleeping in the front passenger seat I could avoid the inconvenience and discomfort of having the gear lever and steering wheel in my way. Naturally, this meant that Kathy had those two items to avoid as much as she could, but she put up with it and survived the discomfort.

After driving many miles, something happened which was to have a lasting and happy effect on our later lives. We pulled into a layby for one of our breaks and, within a few minutes, a car pulling a caravan entered the same layby and stopped in front of us. Within minutes the owners of the caravan, plus their two passengers, had vacated the car and moved into the caravan. The van lights went on and the four people were now sitting around the table at the back of the caravan, eating, drinking copious cups of tea, and laughing and joking. Little did they know that whilst they were merrymaking in the warmth of their caravan, sitting in a car behind them were two people, cold, tired and hungry, with their two children fast asleep on the back seats. It was at that moment that Kathy and I, now green with envy, decided that our tenting days were well and truly over. We saw, over the rainbow, a future for us where there would be no more sitting under canvas in some rain sodden muddy field, lit up only by great flashes of lightning, only to later face the task of dismantling the soaking wet canvas and waiting for it to dry before the journey home. We decided that buying a caravan and heading for the open road was a far more appealing option.

Welcome to the Caravan Club

It was some years later before we could realise this dream. It happened when we were on a trip to

Shropshire to visit Kathy's mother. One day we saw a second-hand caravan marked up for sale for only £300 in the front garden of someone's house. We stopped our car which, by this time, was a Hillman Hunter saloon with automatic transmission. I knocked on the door of the house and, fortunately for us, the owner was in. He gave us a thorough inspection of the van and its history. We were both very impressed with its good condition and after some negotiations, we agreed a price.

I explained to him that we didn't have a towing ball and bracket fixed on our car that was strong enough for towing a caravan and, because we were not local people, we would like to return home to Hampshire and get this necessary safety requirement fitted to our car. We agreed we would return to Shropshire the following week to finalise the deal and pick up the caravan. So, the following Saturday, we returned, complete with a new towing ball and bracket on the car. It was quite exciting to complete the deal, hitch up the caravan and slowly drive away, heading for the open road southwards. I must admit towing a caravan for the first time was a bit of a challenge, particularly negotiating tight corners and roundabouts, but we made the journey of approximately 160 miles safely, delighted with our new purchase.

Part 5
1970s

Chapter 16

Catching the Travel Bug

Events of the Early 1970s

Events which occurred during the 1970s included such varied things, like the 4,000 people who died of an outbreak of Asian Flu throughout the UK in the week ending 2nd January 1970. In London, Karl Marx's grave in Highgate cemetery was desecrated by having swastikas painted on it and was also damaged in an attempt to blow it up.

Aviation history was made when a Boeing 747 aircraft (which, because of their sheer size, were called Jumbos) arrived in Britain. It was three hours late touching down at Heathrow due to engine trouble en route.

On 15th February 1970 Britain lost a man to whom the whole country owes a huge debt of gratitude. I am referring to Air Chief Marshal Hugh Dowding (later 1st Baron Dowding GCB GCVO CMG) who was the man in charge of the RAF's Fighter Command during the Battle of Britain.

Talking of aircraft, Concorde made its first supersonic flight in this decade.

The voting age within the UK was lowered from 21 to 18. The average house price was around £4,900. On the music scene, record players and cassette players were very popular, and the Isle of Wight held its biggest rock music festival which 600,000 people attended. In April 1970, many were surprised to hear that The Beatles broke up.

On the religious side, another surprise came when the Methodists announced that women could become full ministers in its church. Some male cynics quipped that women had been preaching for years without much method, but remember this was before the eventual successful enlightened days of liberation and rights for women came into being.

In the Queen's birthday honours list Sir Laurence Olivier, in recognition of his vast contribution to the world of theatre, was the first actor to be given a life peerage and became Lord Olivier.

It's sad to record that the decade of the 1970s was one of breakdowns of industrial relations throughout the country. There were so many strikes, starting with the British miners who, after refusing a £2 a week pay rise from the National Coal Board, went on strike on 9th January. Power stations were closed and electricity supplies rationed.

To make matters worse, the postmen decided to go on strike for the first time in their history, which began on 20th January.

The troubles in Northern Ireland were still raging. The army used rubber bullets for the first time in both

Belfast and Londonderry, as well as CS gas, in an effort to quell stone-throwing rioters in the Bogside. Sunday 30th January 1972 saw a conflict which killed 13 men and youths, with 17 more wounded. This battle is forever remembered as 'Bloody Sunday'.

One of the biggest changes we witnessed in the UK in 1971 was when the country said goodbye to centuries of dealing in pounds, shillings and pence, and we all tried to understand the new decimal coinage imposed upon us. There were worries that in the confusion some shops and businesses would be marking up their prices, which many did. Older people were hit the hardest, trying to adjust to this dramatic change. Many were reluctant to lose the tanner (sixpence), bob (one shilling), thruppenny bit (a three-penny piece) and the half-crown (two shillings and sixpence). Thinking back to it now, I must admit that when I remember the sheer size and weight of the old one penny coins and consider there were 240 of them to £1, you soon realise why we used to get holes in our trouser pockets!

In June 1970, the tiny island of Tonga (whose Queen Salotte had endeared herself to the British public when, despite the heavy rainfall, she attended Queen Elizabeth's Coronation in 1953) gained its independence from Britain. Also in June that year, Britain, Ireland, Denmark and Norway started talks on their entry into the Common Market. This was a plan for the European countries to form a common trading organisation between one another, with each country retaining all their own independence and sovereignty.

As I write this, that original dream of European unity went, for Britain, badly wrong. It descended into chaos with thousands of unelected politicians making many unpopular decisions which were unacceptable to us. We wanted the right to make our own decisions and our sovereignty.

There was a general election in June 1970 and Ted Heath became Prime Minister, with Alec Douglas Home as Foreign Secretary.

On the sporting front, golfer Tony Jacklin became the first Briton for 50 years to win the US Open when he won the title in Minneapolis. He had already won the British Open and thus joined two of the all-time greats of golf, Bobby Jones and Ben Hogan, as the only ones to have won both Opens in the same golfing year.

A sad loss occurred when Sir Allen Lane died. The name may not be familiar to many, but his brainchild will. He was the man who made paperback books 'famous' by thinking up the idea of calling his books Penguin and, although there are many different paperback books around today, there is only one Penguin trademark.

On 12th September four airliners destined for New York were hijacked. The attempt on one, an EL AL Boeing 707, was thwarted when the crew overpowered the two hijackers, one of whom was killed. The other one, a girl named Leila Khaled, was handed over at Heathrow to the British police. Her arrest caused the hijack of a Boac VC10 and that aircraft, along with the other two hijacked planes, one Swiss and one American, were flown to Jordan where 255 passengers were released before the planes were blown up in the desert, but the hijackers, believed to be members of the Popular Front for the Liberation of Palestine, held 56 British passengers as hostages at a secret location. They were eventually released on 20th September.

Another sad loss occurred when Field Marshal William Slim died. He was the man who led the British 14th Army, the Forgotten Army, throughout the Burma campaign in the Second World War. History books record, quite rightly I might add, the epic struggle in the Middle East when General, later Field Marshal, Montgomery led the 8th Army to victory over Rommel at El Alamein, but the desperate and largely unsung struggle endured by the 14th Army under General Slim, as he was then, in the steamy, unrelating jungles of Burma, were every bit as heroic and deserving of the nation's gratitude.

On another note, on 20th November 1970 missiles were thrown at the stage during the Miss World Beauty Contest in London, claimed to be by members of the Women's Liberation Movement.

Caravanning

Whilst all of the UK troubles and changes were going on, Kathy and I continued our interest in caravanning and joined the Caravan Club. This national organisation was open to any caravan owners to join. It is split into county areas throughout the UK. As we lived in the east part of Hampshire, we became members of the East Hants branch. Joining was one of the best decisions we ever made. Every weekend, members of the many county branches would meet up for a Friday to Sunday rally, which would be held at a convenient site, i.e., a farmer's field, a village hall or school playground local to that area.

Every Saturday evening there would be some diverse options of entertainment which varied from dances in the village or school hall to barbecues on a summer evening where I, along with my guitar and aided by another caravaner who played the piano accordion, would lead everyone in a sing-along session. Another activity which provided much laughter was for participants to visit other designated caravans and play a hand or two of cards whilst enjoying a glass (or two?) of sherry. When suitably refreshed, we would then move on to the next participating couple's van where we would repeat the same act of playing a hand of cards whilst partaking in more sherry-drinking. You can imagine what mayhem sometimes occurred if someone had too many glasses of the amber nectar. The result would be that the individual would be so muddled that he or she would not only have no idea what trumps were, but by this time couldn't care less anyway.

We looked forward to every Friday when we would hitch up our caravan and head off to the designated rally site for that weekend. These weekend breaks were viewed as a welcome rest and a chance to recharge our batteries for the return to work on Monday morning. Chris and Martin were at an age where our caravanning escapades were not for them, so we trusted them to stay at home and not indulge in any wild parties to annoy our neighbours. There were some occasions they would pay us a quick visit on their motorbikes. One of the best aspects of going on weekly caravan rallies was the diverse range of people we met.

It was in 1979 when on a rally in Clanfield, Hampshire, that we were introduced to Terry and Joy Ferry, a lovely married couple who were, not only on their first rally, but also lived not far from us in Fleet. This meeting was the beginning of a strong friendship which lasted for many years especially as they, like us, later also moved to Somerset. Although, our friendship was tragically interrupted when Terry died some years later in 1989. As I write this it is true to say that Kathy and I still remember with great affection the wonderful caravanning days we had with Terry and Joy, and I can assure that those days are still revisited through our frequent contact with Joy.

Starting to Cruise

Kathy and I fondly remember the early 1970s as the beginning of our love for cruising. In 1971, we decided to try a holiday on a cruise liner. Kathy's father had spent a large part of his life at sea. He served as a merchant seaman, a Royal Marine and finally in the Royal Navy, in which he served as a chief petty officer during the Second World War. It was only natural that Kathy was interested in all things naval and very keen to try a life on the ocean wave, even if it was only a holiday cruise.

We took the plunge by booking a six-day trip on a small ship called the Eagle, which acted as a car ferry as well as a cruise ship. The cost of the cruise passage for us was only £45 each for a four-berth cabin on a return trip from Southampton visiting Lisbon (Portugal), Algeciras (Spain), Tangiers (Morocco), and back to Lisbon before returning to Southampton. The whole experience was great value for money. We took Chris and Martin with us and, even though they did sometimes prefer to stay onboard in the swimming pool rather than go ashore on an excursion, it was a big success for Kathy and I and the beginning of a love affair with cruising which we carried on for many years, including celebrating our Silver, Golden and Diamond wedding anniversaries on different ships and visiting many countries around the world.

As the years passed and our finances increased, we upgraded from the small cabin we had aboard the Eagle, to booking an outside cabin with either a port hole window or a larger picture window. This eventually moved up again to the next option, which was to book an outside cabin with a balcony. Just imagine sitting out on your balcony with a drink (or two) on a warm sunny day, gazing at the fluffy white clouds making their own patterns against the azure blue sky as the ship gently glides across the Mediterranean or the Caribbean. To my mind, cruising is a wonderful, leisurely way to travel and explore. You learn so much by meeting different people and seeing their countries and cultures as you visit many of the wonders of the world. It's not only enjoyable, but also very educational and highly recommended.

Two ships we fondly remember are P&O's Canberra and the Royal Princess. We cruised on the Canberra and I remember one sunny afternoon in the Mediterranean when the captain told all passengers he had received a message that there was a bomb onboard the ship and all passengers were to return to their cabins, search thoroughly and to report to one of the ship's officers if they found any suspicious items. This episode came during the height of the troubles in Ireland. We did as we were instructed, found nothing untoward, and the captain announced that nothing had been found. No sooner had this happened when there was a very loud bang akin to a bomb blast. Fortunately, the captain came on the tannoy and allayed any fears by informing us that the bang was not a bomb, but the sound of Concorde breaking the sound barrier as she raced across the sky above our ship. You can imagine what a relief that was.

Hobbies and Mevagissey

As you will already have read, I was interested in sport from a very early age, playing football, cricket, tennis and golf. My youngest son, Martin, followed my sporting interest, but our eldest son, Chris, wasn't particularly interested in ball games. Football or cricket left him cold. He much preferred to sit by a river, canal or pond with a fishing rod and cast his line, with some poor innocent maggot attached, into the water and then wait for a hungry, unsuspecting fish to take the bait.

I suppose you could say Chris had fallen for fishing, hook, line and sinker. Talking of maggots, Kathy had a fright one day when opening the fridge to see a plastic container of wriggling maggots looking at her. You can imagine she was, shall we say, not very pleased.

To Chris, it was sensible to put the maggots in the fridge and thereby have fresh maggots for the hungry fish.

Fortunately, there was a pond within cycling distance from our home in Church Crookham. We bought Chris a new bike (no, it wasn't the Green Flash) and off he'd go with one of his friends on their bikes, complete with rods, maggots, folding seats, a large umbrella, a sandwich or two and drinks for themselves.

It was on such a fishing trip when Chris was hit by a car and sustained a broken leg. He was hospitalised and eventually came out with his leg in a plaster cast and a pair of crutches. The car driver was summoned to court for dangerous driving but was found not guilty.

I remember Chris's incapacity didn't stop us going away on a week's holiday to Mevagissey in Cornwall. There were echoes of Long John Silver as Chris walked along the harbour walls. He only needed a parrot on his shoulder to complete the image.

As a family, we went to Mevagissey many times. We had found a very friendly couple who ran a bed and breakfast business in their house a few miles outside Mevagissey. I remember one trip when Chris and Martin wanted to fish off the harbour wall. Chris caught a fish or two, but Martin couldn't even get a bite. So, unknown to him, when he wasn't looking I took a fish off Chris's line and transferred it to Martin's. He stood there completely unaware until Chris and I shouted out to him, "Look Martin, you've got a bite!" The look of surprise and delight on his face was a joy to behold as this shimmering, fighting tiddler rose from the water into the summer sunlight.

Mevagissey is like so many fishing ports in that you can pay to take a trip on a fishing boat out beyond the harbour wall and try for bigger fish like mackerel, so one day we decided to give it a try. Kathy got on first and I followed with the boys. I deliberately sat with my arms around them just in case one of them might fall over the side of the boat. The water was calm and everything went well as we left the harbour and headed out to the not-so-calm open sea. After about 15 minutes I told the skipper of the vessel that I felt a bit queasy, whereupon he signalled me to move from the back of the boat and take a more stable seat in the middle. At that point I felt so sick that I just had to take his advice and move to the middle. I was so relieved when we returned to the sanctuary of the harbour.

The skipper had caught quite a lot of mackerel and, as we staggered off his boat, he said to us, "How many would you like to take home?" At that moment in time I never wanted to see another mackerel or any fish again, but Chris and Martin wanted to have some so I gave in and they proudly walked through the village back to our car with four or five mackerel tied with string. We took them back to our B&B house where they were gratefully received by our friendly hosts. The irony is that now I love mackerel.

Photography

As well as my interest and partaking in music, particularly trad jazz and skiffle, I also became equally interested in photography. I should point out that this interest was long before the digital age of photography arrived. I bought magazines and read all I could to learn more about the art. I started with a fairly basic Kodak camera, using black and white 35mm film, which was the most popular and easily obtainable at that time. I also bought all the necessary photographic equipment and learnt how to develop and print my own films.

By using the loft of my house in Church Crookham as a darkroom, I was able to develop my films and then print the images of my choice. The only snag with this method was that I had no supply of water, a key element in this process, in my loft. I overcame this by filling a bucket of water downstairs and then carrying it very carefully up a step ladder into the loft. After my developing and printing activities were finished and the prints were emptied into the bucket of water I had taken into the loft, I very carefully carried the bucket back down the ladder and emptied them into the bath filled with water. This neutralised any of the developing fluids used in the whole process. However, Kathy didn't appreciate sometimes coming home from work to be confronted with a pile of photographs lying in a bath of water in the bathroom!

In time, I decided to upgrade my camera and bought a second hand Rolleiflex T Camera. This camera is a classic which, in its heyday, was used worldwide by professional wedding photographers and press cameramen. It uses 120mm film, which gives you square 2 ¼ inch (6x6cm) size negatives, which are about three times larger than negatives from 35mm film. The larger negatives gave a stronger foundation to build on to produce a better resolution and sharper clarity, especially when printing enlargements of any photograph.

I must say, with all due modesty, I, armed with my Rollieflex T (T for Tessar lens) became quite proficient, thanks to the brilliant quality of the camera, particularly the lens. I was even asked to take the wedding photographs for a neighbour of ours whose daughter was getting married at a local church in Aldershot. Not only did I take the black and white photographs and develop and successfully print them afterwards, I also used my own car to drive the bride and groom to and from the church.

Being asked to take someone's wedding photographs was a labour of love for me and, as an amateur photographer, the only charge I made was to ask for my expenses, i.e., cost of films, developing fluids and printing paper, to be covered. This, my first wedding assignment, was successfully repeated a few months later when I was asked by Kathy to take the photographs for a colleague of hers, whose daughter was getting married in Basingstoke. I was happy to accept the request, but there was a problem this time because, not surprisingly, the bride and groom wanted colour photographs, which I was unable to do because I didn't have the right equipment or expertise to print colour. I got over this hurdle by getting a professional photographic library in London to do all the necessary printing. Naturally, using colour film and their services put the cost up quite a bit, but it was worth it. As the day of the wedding approached, I was a bit nervous because of the responsibility facing me, and not knowing any of the people didn't help, but when I saw the church and the surrounding wedding venue, any tension I had was eased by the sight of lush green gardens, tables, chairs and blossoming trees all bathed in the summer sunshine. It was an ideal setting to take colour photographs for any wedding. The big question at that moment in time was whether my efforts would be satisfactory. Thankfully, they were – the quality of the images was brilliant, my expenses were covered and the recipients of the photographs were delighted with the end results.

Another wedding I covered was when one of Kathy's nephews got married in Shropshire. This happy occasion was also captured successfully on Kodak colour film by my trusty Rolleiflex camera. I used the same professional photographic library in London with the same perfect results. As an extra present to the happy couple, I purchased a photo album for them to put their day's memories into.

My camera and I were constant companions and I proudly took it on all our holidays. One holiday I'll never forget was one of the many we've had in the Tyrol region of Austria when, as I got off a coach with my heavy Rolleiflex around my neck, I stumbled and fell a few feet down the side of a hill. Kathy, our two sons, Chris and Martin, plus our nephew, Michael, couldn't help laughing and they recall saying to me, "Dad, one minute you were with us on the coach and the next minute you were disappearing over the edge of a cliff." But, as soon as I stumbled, my first thought was to hold on to my beloved Rolleiflex, which I did.

My Rolleiflex and I were ever-present throughout our caravanning days. Kathy undertook the task of editor of the monthly East Hants magazine, and wrote various articles supplying information and news for the members. I remember we worked together once when I took some portrait photographs of various club members and deliberately cut off the lower half of the print so that only the top part of the head, eyes and hair were visible. These mutilated prints were then inserted into the magazine as a quiz, asking people to identify the subject. I also wrote various articles accompanied with photographs for the national Caravan Club magazine. It's always nice to see your efforts in print.

During these days I was still working at Shell Centre, where it was customary to have a farewell party upon retirement, which was organised and supplied by the company. I was asked, and agreed, to cover many of these happy occasions with my camera. The 10x8 inch photographs my Rolleiflex produced from these occasions were always well-received by the people present.

Finally, the day came when it was time for me to shut the shutters for good on my Rolleiflex. I didn't want to try to sell it as I wanted it to go to a good home and someone who would appreciate its history and quality, so I gave it to my eldest son, Chris, who still has it. These cameras and similar ones are still used by devotees to film photography, rather than digital, and, fortunately, 120mm film is still obtainable if you look hard enough.

Mid-1970s Events

During my happy photography days other things not so pleasant were happening in the UK, such as the conflict between the IRA and Britain, which was never far away. There were many terrible incidents in London and other parts of the UK. The nearest one to us happened when the peace and tranquillity of leafy Guildford in Surrey was shattered on 5th October 1974, when bombs killed five and injured 65.

I remember the big drama in London on 20th March 1974 when Princess Anne, with her husband Mark Phillips, escaped being kidnapped when the Rolls-Royce limousine taking them down The Mall back to Buckingham Palace was overtaken by another car, which forced them to stop about 200 yards from the Palace. The driver of this overtaking car was Ian Ball, a man suffering from a mental illness. Many people witnessed the scene, including three policemen, some protection officers assigned to Princess Anne and other members of the public, including a journalist, a former boxer and two chauffeurs. Despite the stand-off and general pandemonium, the Princess remained very calm throughout the ordeal. Four men were shot, one of them being Inspector James Beaton, one of the protection officers who, despite being shot three times by Ian Ball, survived and was later awarded the George Cross for his bravery.

In April 1974, the government announced big sweeping changes to the Town and County map of England and Wales. Despite their long history of being recorded in the

Domesday Book, certain county and town names disappeared in the biggest reorganisation of local government since 1888. Counties such as Huntingdonshire, Rutland, Cumberland and Westmoreland in England were swallowed up or incorporated either into other counties or given completely new names. For instance, most of the East Riding area of Yorkshire ceased to be a county and was made part of a new county named Humberside. Similar changes also occurred in Wales, for instance, my own birthplace of Bettws Cedewen was in the county of Montgomeryshire, but that county name was changed to Powys.

I also remember 1974 was the year when Prince Charles made his maiden speech in the House of Lords, and thus became the first royal for 90 years to perform that function.

Another man who also made history for a completely different reason in this year was a male streaker who charged onto the hallowed pitch at Twickenham during a rugby match. It was at this event that the crowd found out that a policeman's helmet is more than just protection for his head! This revelation came to light when one gallant officer of the law chased after the streaker and, upon catching up with him, removed his helmet and, to the great amusement of the crowd, used it to cover the intruder's vital statistics. It was said that the match ended with a score of Metropolitan Police 1, The Streaker 0.

Chapter 17

Our Family

Chris

The 1970s brought changes to our family life. Our eldest son, Chris, had developed an interest in motorcycles and wanted to buy one. His cousin, Michael, had bought a Honda CB125s model which Chris also yearned for. I wasn't particularly interested in motorbikes (not as good as the Green Flash), but after a lot of thought and a test drive on Michael's bike, I relented, much to Chris's delight, and we followed Michael's lead and bought Chris a Honda CB125s.

It was during this period of time that Chris had finished his normal schooling days and decided that he wanted to become a chef. He enrolled as a student and began a training course at Basingstoke Technical College in the art of catering. He worked hard and progressed so well that he won the regional final of a cooking competition. This led on to the national final which was held at Westminster College in London. Kathy and I attended and we were so proud to see Chris finish third. After this triumph, he started working for Bateman's Catering

Company as a mobile relief chef. Chris had a natural aptitude for cooking and displayed a refreshing creativity in using enticing names for his dishes such as 'Bateman's Buccaneers' and 'Hawaiian Sunrise'.

Due to the mobile requirements of this job, it was very fortuitous that we had bought Chris his Honda CB125s motorbike. Like most teenagers, Chris loved riding his bike but, like most parents, we always worried about him having an accident. I remember how we could never relax and go to sleep at night until we heard the sound of Chris's bike coming down our road and we knew he was home safely. His love of motorbikes never left him. He, along with many of his friends, travelled all around the UK and Europe on their motorbikes.

During those days, Kathy used a car for transportation to and from work, but even she, who had no great desire for a motorbike, decided a small moped might be a more economical vehicle for her, so she bought a Raleigh run-a-bout. This was a lightweight vehicle combining pedal power with a small petrol tank. Once you climbed on the Raleigh, you pedalled away until you reached a certain speed and then switched over to the petrol option which gave you enough speed to relax, sit back and forget the pedalling. I remember there was one day when Kathy, for some reason, used the car to go to work and I rested my Green Flash bike and borrowed the Raleigh to travel down to Fleet station. It was a frosty morning and the roads were a bit icy. As I approached a T-junction intending to turn right, I slowed down because of the icy road surface, and rather than turn right conventionally and risk sliding on the ice, I went straight across the road, up a dropped kerb, turned right onto a pavement and travelled along the pavement for a few yards to the next dropped pavement that fed back on to the road, and continued my exciting journey to the station. It was a good job this pantomime took place around 6.15am and there was no one around to witness my runabout star turn. At least I didn't come off and tear my trousers, or hit the back of any parked cars!

Little did we know when Chris secured his job at Bateman's that this was the start of a very successful career working as a chef, which, in 1982, led to him emigrating to Canada and securing a job working as a chef in an English pub called *The Jester's Arms* in Stratford, Ontario. In September 1984, he left *The Jester's Arms* and went to work as a banquet chef at *The Waterloo Inn*, situated in Waterloo, also in Ontario. By this time, he had met a Canadian girl named Lois who, like my wife, was also a nurse. They started married life in 1986 and rented an apartment in a town called New Hamburg and later moved to buy a house in Shakespeare, which is about seven miles from Stratford. In 1990, they had a daughter who they named Nicole. Whilst Chris was working hard as a chef, Lois was also working just as hard as a nurse in Stratford. In December 2015, *The Waterloo Inn* was sold and Chris, after working there for over 30 years, left and retired from being a chef.

In 2002, Chris had started his own business alongside his day job, which he called *The British Touch*. His fond memories of home inspired him to start a shop supplying locals and expats with the typical British items they all missed. After a short beginning in Tavistock, the business relocated to Shakespeare where it has remained. Nestled in Shakespeare's old post office and chanticleer store from 2002 until 2004, *The British Touch* then expanded to the premises just next door. In the summer of 2004, the shop moved across the road to a quaint property that gave it the space it needed to grow further, then again for a final time in April 2006 to its current location. Plenty of British treats, groceries, gifts and memorabilia can be found.

Martin

It came as no great surprise when our youngest son, Martin, followed his older brother and became interested in the world of motorbikes. It was 1976 when Chris, aged 17, bought his Honda CB125. Martin was 14 at that time. I recall Martin coming home one day on his pushbike and as he cycled into the rear garden of our house at Church Crookham, he was confronted with the sight of Chris's new Honda CB125 all alone, resting and shining in the sunshine. At that point, Martin had a Walter Mitty moment and, after climbing onto Chris's bike, he drifted into a dream world where he was cruising along the leafy lanes of rural Hampshire and Surrey. This was suddenly shattered by the sound of someone banging on a window. That someone was his mother, ordering him to, "Remove yourself from that unpleasant contraption now!" or words of a similar meaning, but, shall we say, of a little more impolite nature! The sight of her youngest son following her other son down the motorbike route was just too much worry for her at that time.

In May 1978, Martin turned 16 and was legally allowed to ride a 50cc motorbike (called a moped). In March that year, a neighbour of ours had a four stroke Honda ss50 moped which he wanted to sell for £100. He also had a Haynes workshop instruction manual for the vehicle priced at only 50p. We purchased both vehicle and manual for Martin, who spent the next two months reading the manual and tinkering with the bike before he ventured onto the road. As we lived near Aldershot, it was fortunate that Martin was able to practise his skills on an army road in the woods behind our house. He became very proficient with his balance, clutch and throttle control and gear changes. The only downside was that the army road was about half a mile and straight, which limited his chances of practising his cornering skills. However, once out on the open road after his 16th birthday, with L plates attached, he soon mastered that skill, too, and passed his motorbike driving test first time only a couple of months later. Indeed, one year later he also passed his car driving test on his first attempt. Some years after that, he did his advanced motorbike test and passed that first time, too. A hat-trick of firsts. What was his mother worried about? His interest and love for motorbikes grew alongside Chris's, and they travelled together many times around the UK and Europe. I, like many parents, know it can take many years before we learn of some of the escapades our children got up to during their teenage years. It's just as well Kathy didn't know about some of the escapades Martin and Chris got up to on their many motorbike rides! The longest single ride Martin ever did was from his home in Hampshire to Montpellier in the South of France, which totalled 820 miles and he did it all in one day AND it rained all the way! Thankfully, we all survived.

Another activity Martin and Chris got involved with was acting as beaters on some pheasant shoots which were carried out locally. They were happy to receive £4 a day for their efforts, but were a little disappointed when, at the end of the day, the shooters only divided the pheasants between themselves.

After his early schooling days were over, Martin went on to serve a four-year apprenticeship, which included one day a week attendance at Basingstoke Technical College. At the end of the course, he attained a City and Guilds Distinction in mechanical engineering. During his apprenticeship, he was employed as a mechanical engineer at Pilcon Engineering in Basingstoke, part of the Richard Costain Group. After qualifying he was promoted to section manager of the drilling department.

Other jobs he did later in his career included working for two years as a pest control officer for WH Groves in Surbiton, Surrey. This work may have been a somewhat unpleasant task in the eradication of various pests, but it was a necessary job of vital importance for the health of the general public.

As the years passed Martin became interested in the world of finance. He studied and worked hard to gain many professional qualifications and awards, which led to him becoming a qualified financial advisor. These qualifications were put to good use when, in April 1996, he started his own business, opening an estate agency and financial services company called Chapplins. His business partner ran the estate agency, whilst Martin focussed on the financial services side, as well as the business structure itself. Today, Martin has sold his share in the estate agency, allowing him to focus solely on his financial services business which he now runs from home.

Besides Martin's passion for motorbikes, he also took after me in his love for sport. He played football, tennis, squash and golf. He also embarked on many outdoor activities and fundraising challenges, like hiking 130 miles of the pilgrim's path of the Camino de Santiago in northern Spain, a section of the Appalachian Trail in Virginia, USA, and even abseiling down the Spinnaker Tower in Portsmouth. He once joined a crowd of 325 people at Canary Wharf in London to complete an assault course all dressed as penguins, making it the largest human penguin colony in the world. For this feat, he attained a Guinness World Record. However, his greatest achievement was in 2015, when he climbed Mount Kilimanjaro, which is nearly 20,000ft high. This feat, along with all the other charitable work he's done for many deserving causes, has raised over £40,000 and was achieved despite Martin being an asthmatic.

Proud Parents

Both Kathy and I are immensely proud of our two sons for what they have achieved in their lives. They both studied and worked hard and by showing talent, enterprise and great initiative, they eventually owned their own businesses. Chris led the way by having the vision and courage to emigrate to Canada in April 1982 to work as a chef, and he later followed Martin's ambitions of owning his own business.

We have seen our two children marry – firstly, Chris to Lois in 1986, and Martin to Catherine in 1987. Sadly, Martin divorced in 2013, but I'm happy to say he has found love again with Mio. We have also been blessed with three wonderful grandchildren, Chris and Lois's daughter, Nicole, in 1990, followed by Martin's two children; Laura, born in 1991, and Michael in 1995. All three are following their aspirations and dreams as we move deeper into the 21st century. They too are living new experiences and making memories to share in years to come.

Momentarily jumping forward to 2022, which brings both heartache and happiness to our two children. Having been diagnosed with cancer in summer 2021, on 28th March, Chris's wife, Lois, passed away peacefully at home, with Chris, Nicole and Nicole's partner, David, by her side. In contrast, Martin and Mio are due to marry on 1st June in a ceremony in Cortona, Italy.

Kathy and I are very grateful for all the help, kindness, consideration and love our sons have shown us over the years. They have often surprised us by secretly arranging a celebration to mark a birthday, anniversary or for some other event. We are so grateful and appreciative for all the time and trouble they take in arranging these outings. In addition to the above, we owe them an even bigger display of very heartfelt gratitude for the part they played in giving us Nicole, Laura and Michael, our three lovely and caring grandchildren, who are a credit to them.

Alison

She never saw the light of day
Or heard the birdsong calls
The rising of the morning sun
Nor rain that gently falls

The joy of children laughing
Throughout their carefree years
Her world was ever silent
No sound would pass her ears

She never had the gift of life
That comes from up above
Or felt the warmth of life
That comes from mother love

The beauty of the morning mist
The sun upon the dew
Were sights she never witnessed
The child we never knew

No words she ever uttered
No breath she was to draw
Our stillborn baby Alison
The child we never saw

2nd March 1966

Lynn

Our niece, Lynn, is the youngest child of Kathy's sister, Ann, and was born in 1971. Sadly, Lynn lost both of her parents at an early age – her father, John, to a heart attack, and Ann to cancer. She was taken in by one of Kathy's brothers and his wife but, regrettably, they separated, so Lynn came to live with us. All this happened before Lynn had reached the age of three.

Therefore, 1974 was a very busy and different time in the Hodgson household. Our two sons did their best to become instant big brothers to Lynn, and shared a bedroom with each other to allow Lynn to have her own. We all adjusted to life with a three-year-old running around, and in due course took our annual holidays as a family of five, which was tight with a small caravan! We like to think that Lynn's parents, Ann and John, were looking down upon us, comforted by the knowledge that their daughter was being well looked after.

As Lynn grew up, she married and moved away. We've always stayed in touch and have offered the same life guidance to her that we offered Chris and Martin. Lynn currently lives in Scotland and has children of her own.

Part 6
1980s and Beyond

Chapter 18

Carry On Travelling

History was made in the UK in 1979 when Margaret Thatcher, the daughter of a shop keeper from Grantham, Lincolnshire, became the first woman to be elected as the Prime Minister of Britain. Not content with ruffling the feathers of many of the old school diehards in their 'men only' clubs by becoming the leader of the Conservative party in 1975, she beat her rival candidate, Ted Heath, to the top job in UK politics.

Margaret Thatcher was a lady of strong character and resolve. This was brought to the fore in 1982 when Argentina invaded the Falkland Islands. When Argentina invaded these islands, it didn't take long before Prime Minister Thatcher retaliated in defence of the British people living there. After lengthy discussions with the Ministry of Defence and various military chiefs, she instructed that a military task force of British forces should be assembled as soon as possible and sent on the 8,000-mile journey to the South Atlantic to repel this invasion by Argentina. The task force included the Royal Marines, the Parachute Regiment, Scots and Welsh Guards and those fearsome fighters, the Ghurkhas, amongst many others. Air cover and other help was provided by the RAF when needed.

Plans, Disrupted

Whilst Kathy and I were naturally sorry when this invasion happened, we also had a relative personal issue. It so happened that at this particular time we had a cruise holiday booked to take Kathy's mother sailing from Southampton on P&O's Canberra cruise liner to the Canary Isles and Madeira. Unfortunately, and disappointedly for us, the government requisitioned the Canberra and included her as one of the 54 vessels to sail to the Falklands. As Canberra was a cruise liner and obviously not fit for fighting battles, it underwent a complete conversion into a troop carrier which eventually departed from Southampton carrying 9,000 personnel, 95 aircraft, plus fuel and freight.

All of this resulted in Kathy and I contacting our travel agent about this change of plans. Luckily for us, they were able to get us a similar booking and itinerary on Cunard's Queen Elizabeth II (QE2) cruise liner, which was also scheduled to leave from Southampton. Naturally, we were delighted to receive this second chance, but our euphoria was short-lived because a couple of days later, the government stepped in again and this time requisitioned the QE2 to join the Canberra in the task force leaving for the Falklands (she was also converted into a troop carrier).

So, once again, we turned to our travel agent for help. They were very sympathetic and, unbelievable as it may seem, they got us another identical replacement offer. This time it was a booking on the Black Watch, one of the Norwegian Fred Olsen fleet of cruise liners. The only drawback was that the ship didn't sail from Southampton, but from Tilbury in Essex. This meant we had to travel by train to London's Fenchurch Street station then catch another train to Tilbury, then find a taxi to take us to the docks. You can appreciate that this journey with Kathy's mother in tow, plus our luggage, was a bit exhausting, but we made it safely and eventually boarded the Black Watch. Kathy's mother, who incidentally had been cruising with us before on the Canberra, took all of this upheaval in her stride, in fact, she was quite excited by the whole adventure.

The Black Watch was a much smaller ship than Canberra or QE2 and the facilities onboard were not so plentiful or grand. I do remember the dance floor was very small and the necessary music for dancing was provided by only one pianist, but I must say, he was the kind of pianist I like. He just sat at his piano night after night in a very easy, casual style, which I envied very much, and played many of the classic popular 'sing-along' songs written by the likes of George Gershwin, Cole Porter, Irving Berlin, Rodgers and Hart or Hammerstein, Jerome Kern, etc. Kathy and I danced (or shuffled) around the floor whilst her mother watched us from her nearby chair with a smile on her face and a glass of sherry in her hand. The best part of the ship was the restaurant. Being a Norwegian vessel, the food on offer was smorgasbord style, i.e., helping yourself from a lush display of every variety of food one could wish for. It was a wonderful, mouth-watering sight.

When the ship docked at Tenerife on the Canary Isles, we took Kathy's mum on a coach trip around the island which she enjoyed very much. She was such a lovely lady, and it was always a pleasure to see the joy we could provide for her. She never failed to show her genuine gratitude for our efforts.

When we arrived in Funchal, the capital of Madeira, we took Kathy's mum on another coach trip. This one had a special feature – it involved getting off the coach at the top of a steep hill where we found a toboggan and two Portuguese men waiting. These men were there as our 'drivers', responsible for steering the toboggan down the winding road in front of us. They did this by holding on to ropes attached to the toboggan which acted as an aid to hold the vehicle back when, or if, it was necessary. As we descended the winding cobbled road, some of the local children ran alongside the toboggan holding their hands out for money in exchange for the flowers they offered us. Kathy's mum sat there with a look of both apprehension and wonderment on her face. She was glad when she reached the end of this ride unscathed, clutching her flowers and, thankfully, all in one piece.

We visited other islands on this trip and the overall experience was one of great satisfaction. Cruising was such a joy for Kathy's mum and she came with us on another cruise later in life, and we were also able to take her sister, Kathy's Auntie Lily, with us as well. By that time, both of them were in wheelchairs which presented Kathy and I with the task of wheeling them around the ship. Whilst this wasn't always easy, especially in bad weather, we never minded as both of them never failed to show their appreciation. To us it was a labour of love, and we all had some very happy and enjoyable moments on these holidays.

Falklands War

The Falklands War, which had started on 2nd April 1982, finally finished on the 14th June that year when Argentina, after having around 650 troops killed, surrendered. The British Military personnel had 260 casualties, plus three of the Falkland islanders were also killed.

With the conflict finished it was time for our two cruise liners, both of which had been of vital importance to the task force, to return home. The QE2 arrived back in Southampton on 11th June 1982, and the Canberra, which earnt the title of The Great White Whale due to its white colour, arrived back on 11th July.

Kathy and I will never forget the memorable day of Canberra's return home. We were on a caravan rally near Portsmouth on that day. We had a small nine-inch television set in our caravan which I put in our car as we drove down to Southampton to await the arrival of Canberra. There were hundreds of people waiting along the shoreline waving their Union Jacks, which made a wonderful sight against the blue summer sky. There was a great patriotic feeling of warmth and relief filling the air. I switched on our TV which was on the grass in the shade of my car and was able to see Canberra, who had slowly sailed around the back of the Isle of Wight, then came into sight as she entered Southampton water and progressed to the docks and her berth. The sound she received from the rapturous crowd made the welcome home all the more welcoming, with everyone honking their car horns and flashing their lights. It was a magical and proud historical moment in our country's rich history. (This historic sight can be seen online on YouTube – Canberra ship arriving back at Southampton after the Falklands War, July 1982.)

The Canberra carried on cruising for a few years after the Falklands War, and Kathy and I were lucky to enjoy two cruises on her. You only have to mention her name to any lover of cruising and they will immediately respond with their stories and fond memories of this ship. It has a special place in the hearts of all who sailed on her.

Eventually, the time came when this lovely ship reached the end of her voyaging days. She was sold to a ship breaker in Pakistan on 10th October 1997 and finally scrapped on 31st October the same year.

Canada

In late summer 1992, we had another trip to Canada. This time to Halifax, Nova Scotia. It was a welcome shorter flight for us. Kathy and I had a look around the old historic seaport of Halifax for a day or so before joining up with our son Chris and his family, who had driven from their home in Ontario. After a two-day drive, they were happy to meet up with us. Kathy and I rented a car, and together we toured around the Cabot trail in Nova Scotia. It started out as a beautiful day, but as night time came, so did the fog. It was so thick that I recall following Chris's tail lights the best I could as we drove to our accommodation, long since forgetting any sightseeing!

The next day we visited Fortress Louisburg. Having seen so many castles and forts and their historic battles for ownership over the centuries, this one was no different. Upon arrival as I stretched my weary bones from the car, I turned to Chris and said, "Who was the last owner of this one?" He replied, "The French." As we approached the entrance, we were met with some staff dressed in period costume. To get the visit started and attempt to take back control for the English, Chris announced, "Stand aside Frenchies, the English are coming." He heard a response from the staff, "We got some trouble here," but instead of drawing swords, we had some verbal jostling, which was welcomed by all!

We also visited Baddeck, which is located in the lower part of Cape Bretton Island in Nova Scotia. Like so much of Nova Scotia it is very picturesque and is also where Sir Alexander Graham Bell first settled in Canada, after leaving Scotland.

After our time in Nova Scotia, we drove to New Brunswick where we could take the ferry to Prince Edward Island. PEI (as it is known) in Canada is the smallest province and is very lush and green. It's small and quaint, and is also the home of the world-famous fictional character Anne of Green Gables. We toured the area and fondly remember the lobster dinner we had, which is very popular with many tourists. The island also has red soil, almost unbelievable until you see it. It's a deep red-brown, which also grows the great tasting PEI potatoes. Another wonderful place on the island is Cavendish, with its beautiful long sandy beach. It was very peaceful as we walked along to the sound of the surf. We returned to New Brunswick, and a quick trip to see the local phenomenon, Magnetic Hill. You park on the hill and, sitting in your car, you get the illusion of reversing backwards up the hill. It's a strange experience.

We wrapped up another great Canadian trip, parted with Chris and his family as they drove back to Ontario, and we returned our rental car. We flew back to England having created more memories.

Four years later, in 1996, we visited Canada again and Kathy and I decided we would like to visit for a longer period. After some research regarding our travel planning, and organising our UK affairs, we finally made our way to Ontario for three months in the early summer. We found rental accommodation that worked perfectly for us. The owners were often away driving a long-distance transport truck to Mexico, so they were more than happy for us to stay in their house. They became friends, and a year or two later come over to stay with us in England for a holiday. Chris found us a 1978 Pontiac Le Mans car, which was old but serviceable, and became affectionally known as the 'Jolly Green Giant car', due to its sage green livery. Spending this length of time in Canada gave us a much better feel of local living than just the normal two weeks' holiday. We used the car for local trips to Stratford, Goderich and as far as Peele Island, which is three hours away. We also took a coach day trip to Muskoka to visit the cranberry fields which was an eye-opener (we had imagined cranberries grew on large bushes, not on vines in lakes). One of the things we got used to was watching the local 6pm Kitchener news on the television, and I still recall looking for the weather report from Dave McDonald. Funny how a name can stick with you. Our friend Joy flew over from England for a two-week holiday during this time, and stayed with us. We visited Niagara Falls and never fail to be awestruck when seeing this wonderful site. Not wanting to drive any further, we booked a few coach trips. The biggest one being crossing the border to Vermont, New Hampshire, Massachusetts, and New York States. Once we went across by ferry to a place called Sandusky which is in Ohio. The wonderful panoramic views we saw on these particular trips reminded us very much of Austria. We also visited the biggest shopping mall, named Carousel, in Syracuse, New York. The gigantic carousel housed within the complex gives hours of pleasure to the children visiting. We also took Joy to view a newly built housing estate for seniors, somewhere not far from Shakespeare if I remember correctly, which I think had a Scottish name. Anyway, the whole layout was fantastic – houses and bungalows all beautifully appointed with luxury fittings throughout. The whole complex was surrounded by luxurious gardens and a very inviting golf course. We wished we had a place like that near us in England. One of the best places we enjoyed was the Algonquin Park. I have some lovely footage shot on my camcorder of the beautiful colours with added music to fit the scenes.

It was great to be near Chris and his family, as we had a real taste of Canadian living. As we boarded the plane to return to England, it was with mixed emotions. We were sad to leave Canada but looking forward to seeing Martin and his family again. For the next month or so, those mixed emotions continued as, on one hand, we welcomed back all that was familiar to us in England, but missed what had become our second home, some 3,000 miles west.

Chapter 19

Michael

It is an unfortunate fact of life that just when you are enjoying yourselves, something completely unexpected and, in this case, tragic happens.

Kathy and I received a phone call from our youngest son, Martin, on the morning of 4th May 2005, the day before Martin's 43rd birthday, to tell us that his nine-year-old son, Michael, had suffered a major brain haemorrhage during his sleep, which had caused a stroke. We found the utter shock of this unbelievable at first. Even Kathy, with all her years of nursing, found it hard to accept that this had happened to someone so young.

The nightmare had begun when Martin tried to wake Michael for school, only to find that he was floppy and unresponsive. Contacting the emergency services, Martin was told to drive Michael directly to the Royal Surrey Hospital in Guildford. Due to it being rush hour, it was considered this would be quicker than waiting for an ambulance to come to the house. So, off they went, and with Martin constantly flashing his headlights and beeping his horn, he got to Guildford in record time. The nurses were waiting for them at the door.

Many months later, Michael told Martin that, although he had been comatose, he could recall part of that journey in a most bizarre way. He said everything felt quiet and calm, and he was looking down upon the car travelling along and could see his dad driving with himself curled up under a blanket on the back seat. Michael said that the memory was all very clear but was brief. Was this an out of body experience? Had he been near death with his spirit leaving his body? We'll never really know.

Still comatose, Michael underwent a brain scan, all watched on the monitor as the darker patch on the screen got bigger and bigger, and the nurses looked more and more concerned. Apparently, the dark patch was blood that had haemorrhaged onto his brain. It was decided that Michael should be taken without delay by ambulance to the neurological centre at St George's Hospital in Tooting, London. Martin was sent home, some 30 minutes away in the other direction, to get clothes and supplies for Michael. He did this, then drove straight to St George's, only to get there before the 'without delay' ambulance.

Some two hours after arriving at St George's Hospital, Michael's consultant, Mr Simon Stapleton, introduced himself along with his assistant, Susan. It took a few moments for Mr Stapleton to introduce himself and Susan due to his stutter. Martin later told us that it was one of those surreal moments when in a desperate state of mind, humour surfaces when it shouldn't.

Mr Stapleton proved to be a fine consultant, and Martin become very grateful to him.

After the long introduction, Mr Stapleton dropped the bomb: "Michael is in a critical condition with a 50/50 chance of survival." This would improve if he made it through the next two nights. Even then, Martin was told to be prepared for him to endure a disability for the remainder of his life. To what degree, it was too early to say. Such a statement left Martin stunned, speechless and feeling so helpless. The previous night Michael had gone to bed a happy, perfectly healthy nine-year-old boy, and now he faced a very anxious and uncertain future.

After such terrible news, Martin returned home the following day to tell Michael's 13-year-old sister, Laura, of this tragic situation. She asked him directly if Michael might die. Martin could only look straight at her, he could not lie to her and make it sound okay when it wasn't. No words were needed at that moment, Laura simply understood as his stunned look was enough. Martin subsequently said that it was the hardest thing he's ever had to do and hoped nothing in his life would ever be bad enough to eclipse that moment – the moment Laura's direct question hit home, and he felt the full gravity of the situation.

Michael woke after surviving those first two nights. Not in the way you see a patient waking calmly in a Hollywood movie, but instantly crying out in pain due to the pressure the blood on his brain was causing. He remained heavily sedated and slept for many days as the blood slowly dissipated into his body. After a week, he was able to stay awake without being in agony, yet his whole right side was paralysed and he was unable to even wiggle his fingers or toes, he couldn't speak and his vision was blurred.

Over time, and with a lot of physiotherapy and speech therapy, Michael learnt to talk and walk again and his full vision returned.

Once the blood had cleared, a further brain scan revealed the cause of the haemorrhage – an AVM (Arterial Venus Malformation). This malformation occurred pre-birth, where the arteries and veins in his head got tangled up and didn't form properly, causing a weakness which, as blood pressure increases (apparently this can happen whilst dreaming), split open and caused the haemorrhage.

The location in the brain of this malformation was such that it was inaccessible to operate on in the conventional way. The only option was to treat it using a relatively new method called Gamma Knife Radiation (GKR) to zap the nidus of the malformation. No knife is used, just lots of gamma radiation rays blasting through the skull to the centre of the malformation to effectively burn and seal it off from the inside out. The radiation machine was expensive and not many surgeons knew how to use it at the time. Indeed, only two hospitals in the UK had a machine and only one of these was an NHS hospital, in Sheffield.

So, Michael was sent to Sheffield for a consultation. To try and make the overnight stay a little less fraught and add fun, Martin booked one night on a barge on the Tinsley canal, which Michael liked. However, the wait list for Sheffield was too long, so a hospital in Germany was muted that the NHS could use. Preparations begun, but, preferring to keep Michael in the UK, Martin made enquiries to the one remaining UK hospital with a machine, a private BUPA hospital in London called the Cromwell. The cost was prohibitive, so planning started to sell everything they owned to get Michael the treatment he needed – it was better to live in a small house with Michael than a big one without him. However, this turned out not to be necessary as the Cromwell were amazing and somehow got the NHS to fund Michael's treatment. No need to sell up or go to Germany.

Over several years, Michael has undergone the GKR operation three times. The first time was on 26th November 2005 at the Cromwell Hospital, the day after the legendary footballer George Best had died there. Upon entering the hospital, Martin had to ask several gentlemen to stand aside to let them in. He recognised two of the men as George's team mates from Manchester United, Dennis Law and Sir Bobby Charlton.

More than 15 years on, Michael still awaits the all clear. The good news is that today, age 26, although he has little feeling in some parts of the right side of his body which will not improve, he leads a normal life as a self-employed gardener, drives a car and appears as a film and TV extra. Michael has grown up into a very cool, laid back man with an easy-going and likable manner. He has visited Canada, where he stayed with Chris, Lois and Nicole, and has also visited Australia, Tasmania and New Zealand. He recently introduced us to his French mademoiselle, Laurie.

We observed that throughout this terrible ordeal, Michael's big sister was amazing. It would be easy for a teenage girl to feel rejected due to all the attention that was needed to be given to Michael, but Laura showed her love for her brother and was a great support to him. I remember when Michael was born and Kathy and I went to Martin's to see the new arrival, and Laura was sitting on a sofa showing great love as she cuddled her new baby brother. That love carried on and as the years passed it grew into the very strong bond between them which is lovely to see, and still remains to this day.

When our two sons were born I, along with my father, my three brothers and my sister, was pleased that we had boys to carry on the Hodgson family name. In time, this honour will fall to Michael as the youngest male Hodgson of our clan.

Chapter 20

The Bible in the Mud

In April 1918, a British Tommy, my father Herbert Hodgson, was going 'over the top' in battle near Messines in Belgium, when he stumbled into a shell hole and fell upon a mud-encrusted book. He stuffed it into his tunic pocket and climbed out of the hole, when he was then knocked unconscious by a shell exploding nearby. Regaining consciousness later in a field hospital, he examined the book and was amazed to find it was a Bible. He showed it to an officer and asked for his advice. The man, doubting he could find the owner, told him to keep it, adding, "It might bring you luck." Dad did keep it and it certainly did just that. Although he survived the war and lived a very full, interesting and rewarding life, he died in 1974 aged 81, not knowing the identity of the Bible's original owner or what happened to him. One of my brothers remembers Dad holding the Bible and musing, I wonder what happened to the poor bugger who lost this? The mystery continued for the next 92 years and was finally solved in 2010.

During his retirement years, Dad had written his memoirs and due to the help, editing and sheer dedication of one of my brothers, these were published in August 2010:

Impressions of War – The Memoirs of Herbert Hodgson 1893-1974. Although Dad's finding of the Bible was only a small, albeit intriguing, incident in his life changing experiences on the Western Front, the publisher of the book, Geoffrey Hodgson (no relation), was fascinated and wanted to find out more. So, with the help of what looked like a service number written across the closed pages of the book, he trawled the wonderful internet. His painstaking searching finally paid off when he matched the number not to a British soldier as we all had assumed, but to a certain Private Richard Cook from Colac Bay, Southland, New Zealand, who was serving with the Otago Regiment of the New Zealand Expeditionary Force in France and Belgium at the same time as Dad in the Royal West Surreys, and later The Irish Fusiliers. More detective work strongly indicated that Cook had lost his Bible around June 1917 in The Battle of Messines Ridge, the same area where Dad found it some 10 months later! Sadly, it also showed that on 4th October 1917 Richard Cook received two gunshot wounds in another battle near Passchendaele. He informed his parents back home in New Zealand on 7th October that he was wounded in his left hip and right shoulder and was in an army hospital in Etaples, France. Tragically, the next day, he died on a stretcher from loss of blood and was buried in the military cemetery in Etaples.

So, finally, we knew the identity of the Bible's original owner and what had happened to him. We were able to find information of Richard Cook's family and descendants still living in New Zealand and these wonderful revelations were quickly passed on to them. Naturally, they were amazed and thrilled to hear the story. It became known as the 'lost Bible story' in the media in both New Zealand and Britain, with newspaper headlines such as 'British Tommy finds Kiwi's Bible'.

My brother Bernard and I decided we wanted to pay our respects to Richard Cook, so on 8th October 2010, which was the 93rd anniversary of his tragic death, we, along with members of our families plus publisher Geoff Hodgson and his wife, travelled over to the military cemetery at Etaples. Here we met up with two of the fallen soldier's descendants; great-nephew Richard Cook (named after him), who had flown over from Australia where he works, and great-great-niece, Devon Jenkins, from her workplace in Paris. With the Bible and television cameras from Britain and New Zealand present, we held a very moving short service at his graveside. It was a very special and emotional moment and one which we think both soldiers would have appreciated.

After Etaples, we visited many of the battlefield sites including High Wood on the Somme, where my brother and I, responding to a request from the guide of a party of British schoolchildren also visiting the site, had the pleasure of showing them the Bible and relating its story. It was so nice to find youngsters genuinely interested in the story, asking questions and even wanting to touch the Bible. From there we moved on to Messines, where the Bible was lost and found, and then to Passchendaele and Ypres, where we attended the nightly ceremony of remembrance at the Menin Gate. If you haven't seen this yet, I urge you to pay a visit. It is a truly humbling and inspirational experience.

Because Richard Cook had never married there are no direct descendants so we, as a family wanting to return the Bible to its rightful and final resting place, suggested to the Cook family that we donate it to the National Army Museum in New Zealand, where it's very poignant story could be read by future generations of the Cook family as well as other visitors to the Museum. They agreed, so, in March 2011, my brother David and Geoff Hodgson travelled to New Zealand and, in a televised ceremony attended by some of Richard Cook's descendants, the Bible finally came home and was handed over to Colonel Raymond Seymour, Director of the Museum in Waiouru, North Island, New Zealand.

This heart-warming finale to the story came after my father's book was published. You can read the full story, including newspaper and television coverage, still photographs taken at Etaples, and a short video film made by Geoff Hodgson and myself, by visiting www. martlet-books.co.uk, clicking *Impressions of War* and following the links. Alternatively, Google 'Herbert Hodgson, The Bible in the Mud'.

I penned a poem about the story, which I share here:

The Bible in the Mud

The story of this holy book is one of death and blood,
A tale of two brave soldiers and the Bible in the mud.
They never met, these defenders of the Crown,
A soldier from New Zealand and one from London town.

They rushed to join the battle with a loyalty inbred,
To fight for King and country, just as the posters said.
The Empire's men responded as alarm bells briskly rang;
Their kitbag's packed with troubles, they marched and smiled and sang.

But the battlefields of Europe were soon a sea of blood,
As waves of men were slaughtered into a human flood.
The Kiwi soldier lost his book in nineteen seventeen,
It fell into a shell hole near the battle of Messines.

For months it lay, in weary clay, amidst the killed elation,
Of shattered dreams and final screams, this book of revelation.
The Kiwi fell in battle, from wounds he later died,
Because he'd lost the Bible, its comfort was denied.

The British Tommy found it whilst going o'er the top:
He fell into the shell hole and quickly tried to stop.
With arms spread out to ease his body's thud,
He fell upon the word of God, the Bible in the mud.

He put it in his pocket, before a shell nearby,
Exploded with a vengeance that made his senses fly.
He woke up in the hospital, a little worse for wear,
But relief soon overcame him to find the Bible there.

He showed it to an officer – after cleaning off the muck,
The man said, "Better keep it, it might even bring you luck."
The Tommy took the book and carried it with pride,
He made it through to the end, the Bible by his side.

Was this just luck, a mere coincidence?
Or the unseen hand of God, an act of providence.
The Tommy brought the book back to London town;
He tried to trace the owner from a number written down.

But its secret stayed a mystery for ninety years or more,
Until another Englishman decided to explore.

His labours were rewarded through trawling through
the 'net',
He found the Bible's owner in army records set.

The soldier was the Kiwi from far across the sea,
A world away from battlefields, death and misery.
Could it be that now we see God's message all too plain,
That the life he took stayed in this book for another
soldier's gain?

So, rejoice in this their story and proudly hand it down,
Of the soldier from New Zealand and the one from
London town.
Though strangers in the battles, through death and holy
blood,
Are comrades now for ever, through the Bible in the mud.

The website also gives full details and reviews by
eminent people of my father's book which covers his life
growing up and witnessing the social injustices in
London during the early 1900s, his life as a printer
before and after the First World War, his vivid account
of the horrors of trench warfare as a soldier, and his
association with T.E. Lawrence (Lawrence of Arabia)
and printing the original copy of Lawrence's book *Seven
Pillars of Wisdom*, which in turn led to him moving to
the world famous Gregynog Press where during the
years 1927-1936 his fine art book printing earned him
the accolade, 'one of the finest printers of the 20th
century'. Not a bad epitaph for a cockney who described
himself as 'just an ordinary bloke'!

Chapter 21

Mature Years

As my story approaches its mature years, so, of course, does its writer. Like many other people who still see all the wisdom and good there is in our present world, with the vast increases in technology and just the sheer speed of life today, we also yearn for the 'good old days'. I can recall the early 1950s as if it was yesterday. The sounds, news and sights of those days are still vivid to me. Some might say that I am stuck in the past, but I would disagree with that judgement. It's true that as most people get older their memory will diminish a little, but they will also find that they still have fond memories from events they have lived through. The trick to remember is that the lessons they've learnt from those far off days, both good and bad, can be passed on to help establish future decisions. Sadly, in some cases, we charge forward and make the bad mistakes again just in a more modern variation. I have always found humour in many things, especially in times of trouble and hardship, preferring to laugh a little at what life throws at me and remember the lyrics of songs, "Always look on the bright side of life" and "Count your blessings."

Retirement

As I sum up the last part of my story, it seems to have passed so quickly. The mid-1980s to the present day are not in the realm of my heyday so, although more recent, they are perhaps harder for me to recall. However, I can recall the year 1989 for the following reasons: This was when Kathy and I decided it was time for us to retire. We had both worked hard all our lives, Kathy from a student nurse to an SRN, to a part-midwife and, finally, to occupational health nursing sister in a factory in Basingstoke, and my working life started when I left school aged 14. I started out assembling furniture in a factory which I didn't like and left after a week, which was followed by being trained as a cobbler which lasted for four years. I then served my two years' National Service in the Royal Air Force where I was drafted into the signals section and trained as a telegraphist. I then started my job in the communications department of the American Embassy in London which, in turn, led to me joining Shell in 1952 where I continued plying my RAF communications expertise for the next 36 years, starting as a telex/teletype operator before moving up to a supervisor position, and finally retiring from Shell as a unit head of the communications telex department.

So, having decided to retire and, after careful study and discussions, we resigned from our posts and moved from Church Crookham in Hampshire to rural Somerset, settling in the old market town of Chard where we ran a small farm food shop at the Cricket St Thomas Wildlife Park for a couple of years (also the filming location for the BBC series *To the Manor Born*).

Naturally, being in Somerset, the shop sold cider, wines, cheeses, local fudge, biscuits and cakes, as well as various other Somerset-themed wares like tea towels and trinkets. We were lucky in so much as we had a local cider maker named Perry's, who kept us well-supplied. Amongst the many makes of cider we stocked were two with names which always amused the customers – one was called 'Merry Legs' and the other one was 'Cripple Cock' (which had a logo of a chicken on crutches). Many bought these two choices and walked off with their Merry Legs and a merry smile on their faces. Kathy and I really enjoyed our time meeting the many holiday makers and day trippers with their varied personalities. It proved very entertaining and for us it was a world away from our daily commutes and the hustle and bustle of smoky, crowded London. It was a relief, not only for me, but also for Kathy, who had driven daily to Basingstoke for her work and where she'd faced the ever-present big responsibility as the occupational health nursing sister in a factory.

One day whilst we were working at the farm shop, we had a bit of a mishap. I made us a lovely cup of tea, which we enjoyed with the usual satisfaction a classic British cuppa brings. Sadly, after the beverage festivities had concluded, I unplugged the freezer instead of the kettle. The freezer was full of ice cream. You can imagine the sight the next day when we opened the shop! We had to pour it all down the outside drain, and what a frothy mess it was. It would have made a good back drop for a 1950s science fiction film, perhaps something titled, "Ice Cream Invaders from Mars!" Anyway, in due course it was all eventually washed down the drain. Another of life's lessons learnt.

We loved the slower pace of Somerset and talking to the locals with their wonderful West Country expressions. For instance, if you find something which someone is looking for, you don't say, "Here it is" you say, "Yer tiz!" Another expression refers to reversing your car which comes out as, "You gotta back backwards" and another is that many Somerset men refer to their wives as, "My little maid."

Another aspect of Chard we liked was that they had a Light Operatic Society which I, although not an operatic singer, joined and performed in productions such as *HMS Pinafore*, *The Pirates of Penzance*, *Oklahoma!* and other popular 'old time' musicals. Whilst I was doing this, Kathy joined the local WI (Women's Institute) and made many friends by doing so. It gave her a lot of satisfaction, including going on spring and summer holidays which I, along with other husbands, accompanied her to.

We were also very happy to find that living in Chard was only a short drive to the lovely seaside resort of Lyme Regis, where we spent many happy hours searching for fossils. Lyme Regis also had a silver band which occasionally performed from their bandstand situated along the promenade. To sit there on a beautiful summer evening with the smell from the sea vying with the flavour from a bag of fish and chips and a glass of cider in your hand (whilst trying to avoid the seagulls stealing some of your food!) was indeed a very pleasant pastime. Lyme Regis was also featured in the film *The French Lieutenant's woman* with some great shots of its famous harbourfront, the Cobb.

During our time in Somerset, Kathy worked part-time in a care home, and I pursued my love of golf by playing twice a week and also working as a greenskeeper at the Windwhistle Golf Course.

A Blessing to Count

On Saturday 25th January 2014, whilst we were living in Chard, Somerset, something completely unexpected happened. Kathy and I were relaxing at home watching television after returning from a shopping trip to Shepton Mallet when, apparently, I suddenly starting talking what Kathy called, "A load of gibberish." Fortunately for me, Kathy's nursing experience immediately told her that I was having a stroke. An ambulance was quickly summoned to the house where I was carried out and taken to Taunton Hospital. I was later to learn that en route to the hospital I had suffered seizures and 'died' two or three times. Upon arrival at the hospital, I was taken to the appropriate ward for examination. Naturally, Kathy was involved and consulted with the doctor. She told him that our son, Martin, was living in Liphook, Hampshire, and she'd informed him what had happened. A very good friend of ours accompanied Kathy to the hospital and was a great comfort and support to her. This was very fortuitous because there came a point later when the doctor thought it necessary for Kathy to tell Martin to come to the hospital as soon as possible. Martin responded quickly and jumped into his car and headed to Musgrave Hospital in Taunton.

It was around midnight when he left home and it wasn't until he had travelled a few miles when he realised he was low on petrol and had forgotten to bring his wallet. He immediately turned around and raced back home to get said wallet, then headed for the first petrol station. Once this was accomplished, he continued this mercy dash for the hospital. He made the journey safely and was so relieved to find that I was still alive. He was also a great comfort in supporting Kathy at this worrying time.

I must tell you that I was completely unaware of the drama which had been going on around me that evening. It wasn't until the next morning when I awoke to find myself in a hospital bed, completely oblivious as to why I was there. Kathy and Martin were also there (not in my bed of course), sitting in chairs on either side of the bed. It was then that Kathy told me that I had suffered a stroke (a bleed on the brain in my case) at around 10pm the previous evening. Fortunately, I am very lucky that I was born with a calm equilibrium which allowed me to accept this surprising news without any fuss or panic. I felt OK and was grateful that Martin was able to visit and support Kathy.

My body's response to all the necessary treatment I received in the hospital was so successful that I was discharged on the following Wednesday, 29th January, and returned home. Further clinical checks were necessary over the next few months, but this all showed a gradual improvement in my condition. As is usual in such a medical condition as a stroke, my driving licence was revoked for one year which was a blow, but fortunately Kathy could drive and took over. Another blow was being advised to cut back on using my computer. I stuck to all the medical advice I received, including Kathy's, and was delighted when on 24th July 2014 I received a letter from the DVLA (the governing body regarding driving licences) informing me that they had received positive information on my health from my doctor and therefore my licence was now valid once more.

Driving a car again was not the only driving I enjoyed. My love for golf continued and I also enjoyed driving a golf ball from its tee, straight (sometimes!) down the fairway as I tackled playing nine holes of golf again. I received regular medical checks which showed my condition was good and stable. This positive physical progress was attributed to all the sport; football, cricket, tennis and golf, which I had played from the age of 10.

My survival from my stroke was a blessing and I shall always be grateful for the medical expertise I received and, of course, for the love, help and support I received from Kathy, Martin and Chris who, despite being 3,000 miles or so away in Canada, gave his constant support via telephone calls, emails and thought processes. I also received support from other family members and friends. I decided that the only strokes I wanted in the future where ones on the golf course.

Chapter 22

Reflections and Present Day

Reflecting on Changes

Throughout our retirement, the daily pace of the world seemed to really increase. I had used telex machines for many years with my employment at Shell, however, the advent of the internet changed everything. Like so many, I struggled with the understanding of it at first, but my years as a telegraphist helped me. Now, as I write this at age 90, I use the internet daily and appreciate the vast volume of information available in seconds. It's absolutely mind-boggling compared to the limited technology that was available at the start of my story.

Reflecting on Trips

We continued our enjoyment of travelling throughout this period, with quite a few trips to Canada to see our son Chris and his family. Another memory includes trying cross-country skiing for the first (and only!) time, where we spent more time on the ground and getting our long scarves tangled up in bushes than we did on our skis, but we had a good laugh and came to no harm.

We have seen quite a lot of Canada and also the United States of America over the years. As I have said before, our love of cruises has always been there and this period saw us taking many trips by sea.

Reflecting on Photography

My passion for photography has never left me and I still try to take a 'good snap'. The contrast and shades of colours in any picture have always fascinated me. The crisp defines of the foreground and background subjects, coupled with various elements of lighting, can convey such a powerful and timeless image, and can often be very moving. This never-ending desire to capture such an image is always with me. I always appreciate a great photograph. When I turn a page in a magazine and see a quality photograph, I take a second look and admire the work of the photographer.

Moving to Dorset

As I write this, we now live in the small Dorset village of West Moors, near the town of Ferndown. We decided to move from Chard, Somerset, in 2017 to be closer to family. We are only a 30-minute drive from the New Forest in neighbouring Hampshire, and the seaside resorts of Bournemouth and Poole are similar distance drives in the other direction. We are also much closer to our youngest son, Martin, than we were in Somerset.

Another lovely drive through rural England for us is the 40-minute car ride to Clouds Hill cottage, also in

Dorset, near Wareham. This was the retreat of Lawrence of Arabia. Because of my father's connection to Lawrence, you can imagine Clouds Hill holds a special place in my affections.

Covid-19

At this time, the world is still in the midst of the Covid-19 (Coronavirus) pandemic. Before Covid-19 completely took over in March 2020, Kathy and I still managed to enjoy a few short coach holidays. We visited Highclere Castle, near Newbury in Berkshire, where the popular television programme *Downton Abbey* was filmed. We also took other day trips such as visiting Windsor Castle and a boat trip along the River Thames. At the end of 2020, we took a coach trip to Lymington in Hampshire and boarded the ferry crossing to Yarmouth on the Isle of Wight, where we spent Christmas in a Warner's Hotel in Bembridge. Our Christmas stay was very enjoyable with good accommodation and all the usual Christmas good cheer. Naturally, certain and necessary health restrictions due to the pandemic such as social distancing were imposed, observed and appreciated.

In March 2020, the number of people infected with Coronavirus had become so worrisome, coupled with its high transmissibility, that the UK government imposed a compulsory lockdown in order to slow the spread of the virus, and reduce the number of people being admitted to hospital in order to protect our NHS. This meant that everyone, aside from key workers such as hospital and supermarket staff, had to stay in their homes, only leaving to buy food and essentials and for a short period of exercise per day. Throughout 2020 and 2021, the people of the UK experienced several lockdowns and many restrictions, particularly to their work and social lives.

As I watched the news today I, like so many, have great faith in our modern-day scientists and their dedicated work on vaccines. As I bring my story to a close, I am pleased to say that mass vaccination programmes have begun all over the world. This pandemic has taken a huge toll on this Mother Earth, many lives have been lost and much suffering has been endured. Many scheduled surgeries have been cancelled as hospitals struggle to deal with Covid-19. Fortunately, vaccines to protect against the virus have been developed, and the government have introduced many vaccination centres in an effort to combat this pandemic. Being in our 80s and therefore more vulnerable to becoming seriously ill if infected with the virus, Kathy and I have had all the vaccinations currently available. With the roll out of vaccines across the globe, I hope that we have now turned a corner. Time, as always, will tell.

As I lay my pen to rest, it is with a heavy heart, as the world learnt of the passing of Her Majesty Queen Elizabeth II on 8th September 2022, having reigned for 70 years. I join with millions of people all around the world in thanking her for her outstanding life of service to Great Britain and the Commonwealth, for her positive influence and the inspiration she provided to so many throughout her 96 years.

Conclusion

The changes from the start of my life in rural Wales to today are astonishing. Technology, the speed of communication, travel, medicine and our perceptions have all vastly changed.

My enquiring mind wonders with both amazement and fearful anticipation what the next 100 years of *Ivor's Insights* would look like. Although I won't be around to report on the next century, I hope that you, my family and friends, enjoy the wonders this world has to offer and create precious memories to, in time, share with your own families, as I have done here. Writing my story has truly been a labour of love for me, and I hope that you have enjoyed reading it. I can't help reflecting on the fact that my love of using our wonderful English language to stir the mind all started on that beautiful summer's day back in 1945, when I was 14 years old and on summer camp with the Boys' Brigade. If my story has in any way made you consider writing yours, then I offer these words for your consideration as a starting point:

Talk to your parents before it's too late,
Write down the stories they can relate.
Do it now before you forget,
Have precious memories, not sad regrets.

Ivor Hodgson
September 2022

Account of All Our Cruises

1. Eagle: Lisbon, Vigo, Algerciras, Tangier 1973
2. Canberra: Lisbon, Madeira, Canaries 1981
3. Black Watch: Lisbon, Madeira, Canaries 1982
4. Sea Princess (Victoria): Lisbon, Madeira, Canaries (won)
5. Royal Princess: Maiden Voyage, Miami 1984
6. Sea Princess (Victoria): West Indies
7. Victoria: West Indies
8. Victoria: West Indies
9. Canberra: Lisbon, Madeira, Canaries 199?
10. Victoria: Norway, Iceland, Ireland 199?
11. Rhapsody of the Seas: Alaska 199?
12. DFDS: Denmark 198?
13. Dolphin: Key West, Bahamas 198?
14. QE2: New York 198?
15. QE2: New York, Boston 198?
16. Oriana (Millenium): Vigo, Gibraltar, Barcelona, Majorca, Canaries 1999
17. Aurora: Azores & USA 2002
18. Aurora: New York, Boston, Halifax 2002
19. Arcadia: Fly to Barbados, Mayreau, Dominica, Antigua 2003
20. Adonia: Gib, Port Said, Limasol, Marmaris, Pireaus, Sardinia, Ibiza, Malaga 2003

21. Oceana: Lisbon, Vigo, La Rochelle and Guernsey (missed due to weather) 2004
22. Aurora: Gibraltar, Med, Greek Islands, Venice, Croatia, Palma 2006
23. Brilliance of the Seas: Barcelona, Alexandria, Eastern Med 2009
24. Island Escape Thomson: From Tenerife, Canaries, Madeira and Agadir, Morocco 2010
25. Artemis: Around Britain 2011
26. Independence: Canaries 2012
27. Thomson Celebration: Canaries 2014
28. Ryndam: Norway (ship dreadful, would never sail with Holland America again!)
29. QE2: Southampton to New York (with two weeks in Canada after) 2015
30. QE2: New York to Southampton 2015
31. Britannia: Gibraltar, Barcelona, Palma, Ibiza, Cadiz, Lisbon 2016
32. QE2: New York 2016
33. Adonia P&O: Round Britain, mainly Ireland and Scotland 2017
34. Oceana: (Christmas) Canaries, Lisbon, Madeira (60th wedding anniversary) 2018

Some Kind Words About My Articles in
The British Touch Newsletter:

Ivor, thank you for your 'Insights', each edition of which was not only anticipated, but read with relish and admiration. Wonderful glimpses into the social history of our time. Thank you. I trust you will continue to write. Keeping track of the events, both large and small, with one's perceptions of the same is an invaluable resource to the generations to come.

Robin & Paul
Saint Thomas, Ontario, Canada

Through his insights, Ivor invited all of us on his personal journey of experiences, thoughts and passions down his road of life. His writings provoked within us memories of shared times or familiar events, thus allowing us to relive our own lives during this period. We feel very privileged at being invited into sharing not only his own life stories, but those of his family. Well done my friend, and thanks for the memories.

Norm & Barb
Kitchener, Ontario, Canada

CPSIA information can be obtained
at www.ICGtesting.com
Printed in the USA
LVHW020843251022
731488LV00008B/102